HISTORY
HF
FIRSTHAND

D0976263

Sixties Counterculture

Stuart A. Kallen, *Book Editor*

David L. Bender, *Publisher*
Bruno Leone, *Executive Editor*
Bonnie Szumski, *Editorial Director*
Stuart B. Miller, *Managing Editor*
David M. Haugen, *Series Editor*

Greenhaven Press, Inc., San Diego, California

Other Books in the History Firsthand Series:

The Civil War: The North
The Civil War: The South
The Great Depression
Japanese American Internment Camps

Every effort has been made to trace the owners of copyrighted material. The articles in this volume may have been edited for content, length, and/or reading level. The titles have been changed to enhance the editorial purpose.

Library of Congress Cataloging-in-Publication Data

Sixties counterculture / Stuart A. Kallen, book editor.
    p. cm. — (History firsthand)
    Includes bibliographical references and index.
    ISBN 0-7377-0407-1 (lib. bdg. : alk. paper) —
    ISBN 0-7377-0406-3 (pbk. : alk. paper)
    1. United States—History—1961–1969. 2. United States—
Social conditions—1960–1980. 3. Subculture—United States—
History—20th century. 4. Radicalism—United States—History—
20th century. I. Kallen, Stuart A., 1955–   . II. Series.

E841 .S53 2001
973.923—dc21   00-029377
                                                    CIP

Cover photo: Maury Englander/FPG
The George Meany Memorial Archives, 207
Library of Congress, 24, 36, 176
National Archives, 14, 93

Contents

Chapter 1: Seeds of the Counterculture: The Early 60s

Chapter 2: War Protesters

Chapter Preface

1. "Vietnam Day" Protest in Berkeley
by Jerry Rubin
As the war in Vietnam grew in scope so did the actions of the antiwar protesters. In October 1965 tens of thousands of protesters marched in the Vietnam Day protest in an attempt to close down the Oakland Army Terminal where recruits were shipped out for Vietnam.

2. Vietnam Veterans Against the War
by Richard Stacewicz
There were many groups with different agendas who opposed the war in Vietnam. Perhaps those with the most insight into the horrors of the war were the Vietnam Veterans Against the War (VVAW), a group made up of former soldiers who had seen action in Vietnam and who often led antiwar demonstrations.

3. Refusing to Serve
by David Harris
After serving as student body president of Stanford University in 1966, David Harris became a national leader in the antiwar movement. When he returned his draft card to the government, he was forced to serve two years in a federal penitentiary.

4. Violence at the Democratic Convention
by Tom Hayden
In 1968, as the Democrats assembled in Chicago for their presidential convention, thousands of people from across the country descended on the city to protest the war in Vietnam. They were met by eleven thousand Chicago police, six thousand National Guard troops, and seventy-five hundred fully armed U.S. Army soldiers.

Chapter 3: Hippies and the Psychedelic Revolution

Chapter Preface

Foreword

In his preface to a book on the events leading to the Civil War, Stephen B. Oates, the historian and biographer of Abraham Lincoln, John Brown, and other noteworthy American historical figures, explained the difficulty of writing history in the traditional third-person voice of the biographer and historian. "The trouble, I realized, was the detached third-person voice," wrote Oates. "It seemed to wring all the life out of my characters and the antebellum era." Indeed, how can a historian, even one as prominent as Oates, compete with the eloquent voices of Daniel Webster, Abraham Lincoln, Harriet Beecher Stowe, Frederick Douglass, and Robert E. Lee?

Oates's comment notwithstanding, every student of history, professional and amateur alike, can name a score of excellent accounts written in the traditional third-person voice of the historian that bring to life an event or an era and the people who lived through it. In *Battle Cry of Freedom*, James M. McPherson vividly re-creates the American Civil War. Barbara Tuchman's *The Guns of August* captures in sharp detail the tensions in Europe that led to the outbreak of World War I. Taylor Branch's *Parting the Waters* provides a detailed and dramatic account of the American Civil Rights Movement. The study of history would be impossible without such guiding texts.

Nonetheless, Oates's comment makes a compelling point. Often the most convincing tellers of history are those who lived through the event, the eyewitnesses who recorded their firsthand experiences in autobiographies, speeches, memoirs, journals, and letters. The Greenhaven Press History Firsthand series presents history through the words of first-person narrators. Each text in this series captures a significant historical era or event—the American Civil War, the

Great Depression, the Holocaust, the Roaring 20s, the 1960s, the Vietnam War. Readers will investigate these historical eras and events by examining primary-source documents, authored by chroniclers both famous and little known. The texts in the History Firsthand series comprise the celebrated and familiar words of the presidents, generals, and famous men and women of letters who recorded their impressions for posterity, as well as the statements of the ordinary people who struggled to understand the storm of events around them—the foot soldiers who fought the great battles and their loved ones back home, the men and women who waited on the breadlines, the college students who marched in protest.

The texts in this series are particularly suited to students beginning serious historical study. By examining these first-hand documents, novice historians can begin to form their own insights and conclusions about the historical era or event under investigation. To aid the student in that process, the texts in the History Firsthand series include introductions that provide an overview of the era or event, timelines, and annotated bibliographies that point the serious student toward key historical works for further study.

The study of history commences with an examination of words—the testimony of witnesses who lived through an era or event and left for future generations the task of making sense of their accounts. The Greenhaven Press History Firsthand series invites the beginner historian to commence the process of historical investigation by focusing on the words of those individuals who made history by living through it and recording their experiences firsthand.

Introduction

The Decade of Turmoil

The years that made up the 1960s were some of the most exciting and turbulent years in American history. The post–World War II baby boomers grew up, a president and prominent civil rights leaders were assassinated, the Vietnam War dragged on for years, millions of Americans openly experimented with psychoactive drugs, and rock and roll music became a cacophonous national anthem.

It seemed that there was group action in the streets almost every day. Angry students took over campus administration buildings in protest of various social problems. Anti–Vietnam War demonstrations turned into full-scale street battles. Riots exploded in big-city black neighborhoods across the nation. For average Americans—or the "silent majority" as President Richard Nixon called them—it appeared that the United States was collapsing into chaos.

While America never devolved into anarchy as it often seemed that it would, the passionate protests and the experimental lifestyles did change the country—and the world.

In the Beginning

On New Year's Eve 1959, no one could have envisioned how much the basic fabric of the United States would change by New Year's Eve 1969. As the 1950s drew to a close, a 70-year-old former World War II general, Dwight D. Eisenhower, was president. At the time, Eisenhower was the oldest man to have ever lived in the White House, and he had suffered a major heart attack and a minor stroke during his two terms in office. He was more often seen waving to photographers from a golf course than speaking from a presidential podium.

But Americans had little reason to pay attention to their ailing president. America was a country on the move. Gas-guzzling automobiles plied brand-new freeways that were built across America. The freeways connected brand-new suburbs in which most of the houses looked virtually the same.

On television, the ideal American family was the so-called "nuclear family" made up of a mother, a father, and several children. The great African American rockers of the mid-fifties such as Little Richard and Chuck Berry had been replaced on the radio by squeaky clean teen idols like Fabian and Paul Anka who crooned sugary, sanitized "white" versions of rock music.

Since World War II America had become a very wealthy country. According to David Farber in *The Age of Great Dreams: America in the 1960s:*

> Between 1946 and 1960 every indicator of national wealth and prosperity had soared. The stock market entered the new year more than twenty times higher than it had been in the Depression year of 1932. The gross national product had increased about 250 percent since the end of World War II, and the median family income, adjusted for inflation, had almost doubled. What those numbers meant for a majority of Americans was a material life, in world-historical terms, of incredible abundance. In 1960, America was the richest nation the world had ever seen. Americans, though not without some doubts, expected that boom times would just keep on rolling. Economic wealth—coupled with the faith that economic growth would continue and the fact that for many years it did—shaped the 1960s like no other single factor.[1]

The end of World War II and this new flush of prosperity fueled what later became known as the Baby Boom. The number of births climbed 19 percent in 1945, 12 percent in 1946, and boomed again in the early fifties. In fact, between 1948 and 1953 more babies were born than in the previous thirty years. By 1964 thirty million babies had been born and the largest age group in America was comprised of seventeen year olds. By 1965, 41 percent of all Americans would be under the age of twenty.

On New Year's Day 1960, most of these baby boomers had yet to finish high school. College campuses were quiet places filled with studious young adults who wore short hair, and conservative clothing, and rarely argued over basic political philosophies. In fact, a 1957 survey found that 59 percent of students felt their teachers might have ideas that were too radical and that they should be carefully watched. Forty percent felt that the Communist party should be outlawed and radicals of any sort should be barred from teaching. A majority believed that men who refused to join the army and fight for their country should be expelled from the United States.

The fifties generation was so passive, in fact, that Clark Kerr, chancellor at the University of California at Berkeley, stated: "Employers are going to love this generation. They are going to be easy to handle. There aren't going to be any riots."[2]

Chancellor Kerr had no idea that he would later come to rue his remark about passive college students, when in 1964, a group of 1,500 students stormed the UC Berkeley campus administration building and occupied it for more than 24 hours.

Rumblings of the Counterculture

The turmoil of the sixties had its roots in a series of seemingly unrelated events that took place in the 1950s. In 1954 in Southeast Asia a civil war divided the formerly unified Vietnam into two countries—North Vietnam and South Vietnam. Within a decade hostilities between those two countries would drag the United States into the Vietnam War. In Cuba, 90 miles off the coast of Florida, the authoritarian government of Fulgencio Batista was overthrown in 1959 by revolutionaries Che Guevara and Fidel Castro who began taking monetary and military support from the Communist Soviet Union. By the mid-sixties Che Guevara would become a socialist hero to thousands of American college students who were dedicated to revolutionary change in the United States.

In the Deep South Martin Luther King Jr., a young African American minister, was making headlines leading non-violent protests against segregationist laws that barred black people from using the same restaurants, city buses, bathrooms and other facilities as whites. As the sixties progressed, white Americans would adopt Dr. King's tactics in order to protest the Vietnam War.

In Washington, D.C., the Central Intelligence Agency (CIA), in a desperate fear that the Soviets were mastering "mind control" using drugs, set out on an ambitious campaign to explore the psychedelic effects of LSD (lysergic acid diathymalide). Beginning in 1953, the CIA had funded a program called MK-ULTRA whose mission was to give LSD to unsuspecting soldiers and citizens to determine the mind-bending influence of the drug. By 1960, the government was paying college students at Stanford University in California $25 to take LSD and explain their experiences to researchers. One of those students, Ken Kesey, would begin handing out free LSD to hundreds of soon-to-be hippies in San Francisco and elsewhere, beginning a psychedelic revolution unprecedented in history.

Political Awakenings

While Eisenhower, a conservative Republican president, had run the country throughout most of the fifties, in 1960 John F. Kennedy (JFK) was elected president. At the age of forty-three, the handsome and wealthy Kennedy was the youngest person to be elected president. Kennedy's youthful idealism seemed to inspire the entire nation. He established the Peace Corps, in which thousands of young people volunteered to help the poor in third-world countries. The president also promised that Americans would walk on the moon before the end of the decade.

The election of the liberal Kennedy also seemed to awaken the political yearnings of the baby boomers who were just coming of age. Students founded an alphabet soup of political groups, including SDS, or Students for a Democratic Society, which was formed in Ann Arbor, Michigan, in 1960 and was dedicated to civil rights and other left-wing political causes. SNCC, or the Student Nonviolent Coordinating Committee, was an interracial group that was fighting racism in the South. In 1964, students at the University

The election of Democratic president John F. Kennedy in 1960 reflected political change. His youthfulness and lofty ideals made him an inspiration to the American public.

of California at Berkeley had formed the FSM, or Free Speech Movement, to oppose campus censorship.

The struggle for civil rights in the South ignited the passions of all of these various organizations and gave them common ground on which to unite. SDS member Tom Hayden writes about the convergence of these idealistic organizations in his book *Reunion:*

> On February 1, 1960, the historic events of the decade unexpectedly began. Four unknown black students staged a sit-in at a segregated lunch counter in Greensboro, North Carolina, and started what was soon called "the movement." From that point until the August 1963 [civil rights] march on Washington [led by Martin Luther King Jr.], there commenced an era of unmatched idealism in America. The student civil rights movement took the moral leadership, showing how values could be translated into direct action. Students across the country became agents for social change on a larger scale than ever before. A new, more hopeful, presidency was in the making. In this brief moment of time, the sixties generation entered its age of innocence, overflowing with hope.[3]

After observing "the movement" and marching with African Americans, white middle-class college students soon began to take action in their own lives. The first student revolt of the decade erupted at the University of California at Berkeley on September 30, 1964, when eight students were suspended for handing out leaflets on campus property and raising money for civil rights groups. From this incident the Free Speech Movement was born, which culminated on December 3 when 800 students were arrested for staging a massive sit-in at Sproul Hall. The arrest was the largest in California history, and many members of the FSM later went on to protest the Vietnam War.

Between the civil rights march in Washington in 1963 and the occupation of Sproul Hall the following year America experienced an unparalleled tragedy when President John F. Kennedy was assassinated in Dallas on November 22, 1963. Although the alleged shooter was said to be a loner named Lee Harvey Oswald, a majority of Americans did not believe the official version of events. In one shocking moment, the idealism of the early sixties seemed to be replaced by a general cynicism and distrust in the government. Kennedy's death was believed by many to be a conspiracy involving any number of players including the Soviet Union, Castro loyalists, the CIA, or even Lyndon Baines Johnson, the man who replaced Kennedy as president.

Revolutionary Musical Changes

Throughout the Thanksgiving and Christmas holidays in 1963 America mourned for their fallen president. As the new year dawned, the sadness of the previous autumn was driven away when the music of the Beatles arrived in America. By January 1964, "I Wanna Hold Your Hand," was blasting out of millions of record players and car radios. In February, when the Beatles appeared on the popular *Ed Sullivan Show,* more than half the television sets in America were tuned in to watch. And the Beatles introduced more than just well-crafted, energetic rock songs. They also had what was considered at the time to be long hair. Almost overnight, tens of thousands of American males let their hair grow long and picked up guitars to form their own Beatles-inspired rock groups.

As the lilting harmonies of the Beatles became the soundtrack for the sixties, folk musicians such as Joan Baez and Bob Dylan popularized so-called protest music. As *Time* magazine wrote: "Suddenly . . . the shaggy ones are high on a soapbox. Tackling everything from the Peace Corps to . . . foreign policy to domestic morality, they are sniping away in the name of 'folk rock'—big-beat music with big-message lyrics."[4]

Bob Dylan's electrified songs of social and political commentary were quickly imitated by a wide range of other groups including the Beatles. And when Dylan gave the Beatles marijuana for the first time, the mid-sixties music boom took on an original, layered, and introspective tone. When Dylan sang "Everybody must get stoned," on his 1965 "Blonde on Blonde" album, for the first time, drug use was openly encouraged in the mass media.

Meanwhile, African Americans, enjoying the first benefits of the civil rights movement, began to top the pop charts formerly reserved for white artists. The bluesy soul records of Aretha Franklin, Otis Redding, James Brown, The Temptations, the Four Tops, and others were eagerly snapped up by black and white teenagers alike, and helped inspire the move toward integration and black acceptance in white society.

Bob Dylan first became popular on the East Coast, and soul music was a phenomenon of Midwest industrial towns such as Detroit. On the West Coast, another new school of music was formed by rock bands in San Francisco who ingested LSD for drug-inspired jams. Jefferson Airplane's "White Rabbit," with its obvious drug references, was the first hit from a San Francisco band. The alcohol- and acid-fueled blues of Janis Joplin also topped the charts. Jimi Hendrix, who first became popular in England, was the kaleidoscopic godfather of psychedelia, while the dark revolutionary lyrics of lead singer Jim Morrison fueled riots at dozens of Doors' concerts.

With such a cornucopia of new and vibrant music available—and such negative news of war in the papers—rock and roll and the counterculture lifestyle became almost a religion for some. In *20 Years of* Rolling Stone: *What a Long, Strange Trip It's Been,* singer-songwriter David Crosby, formerly of the Byrds, offered his opinion on this phenomenon:

> On one side you got war, degradation, death, submission, guilt, fear, competition; and on the other hand you got a bunch of people lyin' out on the beach, walking around in the sun, laughin', playin' music, makin' love and gettin' high, singin', dancin', wearin' bright colors, tellin' stories, livin' pretty easy. You offer that alternative to a kid, man, and the kid ain't crazy yet. I think that they've probably lost the majority of their kids by now.[5]

Escalating the War in Vietnam

The war, death, and fear that Crosby was talking about was the ever-growing American involvement in Vietnam. When John F. Kennedy became president in 1960, he began to send "advisers" to South Vietnam to train their small, disorganized army in their fight against the Communist North Vietnamese. According to Farber: "Kennedy came into office with the belief that America could and should shape the destiny of the world's developing countries."[6]

By 1962, the number of Americans in Vietnam had grown to 12,000 and the government was spending half a billion dollars a year to support the South Vietnamese army in their fight against the Vietcong, also known as the National Liberation Front or NLF. The United States began to send American pilots to accompany South Vietnamese pilots on bombing missions.

These pilots also used a weapon called napalm to burn jungles, villages, and people. Napalm, a mixture of gasoline and a gelling agent similar to that used in dish soap, was dropped in bombs. It adhered to whatever it touched, burning with a very intense heat. Although napalm was used in World War II and the Korean War, its use as a major weapon in Vietnam came to epitomize the evil of the war to protesters who often mentioned it in their anti-war tracts.

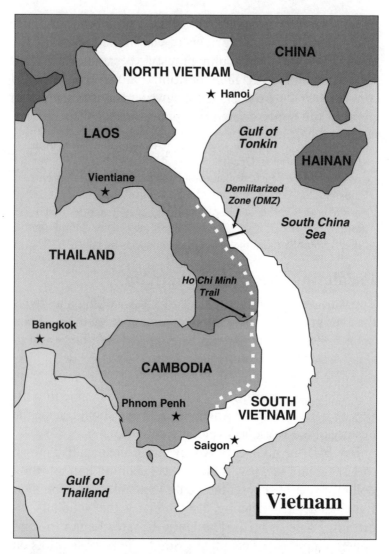

The United States also aided in dumping tons of toxic defoliant called Agent Orange on the jungle to destroy the hiding places of the Vietcong. In spite of these efforts, the NLF remained in control of much of the South Vietnamese countryside.

When Kennedy was assassinated and Johnson became commander-in-chief, the new president was well aware that he could not drastically change policy in Vietnam because he didn't want to appear weak to Chinese and Soviet leaders. He told one adviser: "They'll think with Kennedy dead [the United States] has lost heart. . . . The Chinese. The fellas in [Moscow]. They'll be taking measure of us."[7] At the same time, Democrats in general and Johnson in particular did not have the political will to face accusations from their Republican rivals in Congress that they "lost" South Vietnam to the Communists.

So with political rather than strategic goals in mind, Johnson began to escalate the war. Richard Stacewicz explains in *Winter Soldiers:*

> By mid-1964, the American role in Vietnam had changed dramatically. The Johnson administration . . . was looking for a way to increase military involvement without seeming to contradict Johnson's campaign promise to keep the nation out of a "hot war" in Vietnam. . . . Johnson needed to present the war in Vietnam as a defensive measure, and he found a way to do this in August 1964, when United States naval cruisers in the Gulf of Tonkin were attacked—or were said to have been attacked (there was little if any evidence that the attacks actually took place). Johnson characterized the alleged attacks as an assault on American sovereignty, and Congress thereupon gave his administration what amounted to a blank check, the "Tonkin Gulf Resolution": the American military presence in Vietnam could be escalated without any formal declaration of war. As a result, the war entered a new and much more dangerous phase.

> With this new mandate in hand . . . Johnson began a bombing campaign called "Rolling Thunder" in the spring of 1965. Both North and South Vietnam were bombed, although until then direct military involvement by the North Vietnamese had been negligible. Along with this dramatic increase in the air war, there was also an increase in American ground personnel. American ground forces charged with actually engaging in battle had been introduced into the country in March 1965. With the massive buildup in troop strength that followed, the United States began to rely on citizen-soldiers. In the summer of 1965, Johnson authorized the conscription of 35,000 men monthly. The escalation of United States forces continued without interruption during the next three years, so that by the end of 1967, about 500,000 Americans were stationed in Vietnam. The average age of the American conscripts was nineteen.[8]

Resisting the War

By 1969, more than 14,350 Americans had been killed in Vietnam and 323,600 had been wounded. That same year over 250,000 Americans marched in Washington, D.C., to protest the war. And there was one major reason many people chose to protest the war in Vietnam—the draft board.

All American males between the ages of 18 and 35 were required to register with the Selective Service Administration and could be drafted into the army at any time. The draft board granted deferments to college and graduate-school students, which meant that much of the force in Vietnam was composed of minorities and working-class white people who could not afford college. With nearly three million men, and some women volunteers, needed by the military, thousands of men were drafted every year. The debate over the war had so alienated teenagers with anti-war beliefs from parents who supported the action, that the term "generation gap" was coined to describe the problem.

As the war dragged on, the anti-war movement was growing to include millions of Americans—many of whom had formerly supported the war. Unlike wars in previous decades, the Vietnam War was the first to be televised. Almost every evening the national news featured uncensored footage of burning villages, dead American soldiers, terrified Vietnamese peasants, and other horrific images. In addition, the drugs that were becoming rampant in the United States were also spreading among soldiers in Southeast Asia. Some demoralized soldiers who were slogging through the rice paddies of Southeast Asia also began to question their mission.

Make Love, Not War

While bombs, napalm, and destruction rained on rural villages in Vietnam, half a world away in San Francisco, the drugs of a new counterculture were drastically changing the personalities of thousands of people. As an international port, San Francisco had always been a place where off-beat characters had gathered. By the late 1950s, San Francisco was home to dozens of beatnik poets and writers such as Allen

Ginsberg, Jack Kerouac, and others. When LSD began seep-
ing out of laboratories and research institutes, the black-clad
poets who smoked marijuana, drank coffee, and read poetry
suddenly transformed into wild-eyed, long-haired hippies (a
term coined by a reporter from the old term "hipster"). The
beats abandoned their berets, and dressed, according to au-
thors Jane and Michael Stern in *Sixties People*,

> [in] a riotous getup of thrift-shop Victorian shawls, low-slung mod
> bell-bottom [pants], and mind-blowing paisleys. They combined
> bowler hats, fringe jackets, and western boots: they carried fop-
> pish canes. Their hair was wild and unruly, their beards full in-
> stead of neatly trimmed.[9]

LSD was the drug of choice among these hippies. The
drug had two enthusiastic salesmen, Dr. Timothy Leary and
Ken Kesey, who championed the virtues of chemically in-
duced mind expansion to the American masses. Leary, a
clinical psychology professor at Harvard University in
Massachusetts, began his psychedelic experiments in Mex-
ico in 1960 with psilocybin mushrooms. In *The Politics of
Ecstasy,* Leary wrote that he felt himself "being swept over
the edge of a sensory Niagara [Falls] into a maelstrom of
transcendental visions and hallucinations. The next 5 hours
could be described in many extravagant metaphors, but it
was above all and without question the deepest religious experience of my life."[10]

When Leary returned to Harvard he created an enormous
controversy when he began psilocybin experiments on hundreds of student volunteers, and began experimenting with
many other psychoactive drugs including peyote, marijuana, mescaline, and LSD. By 1963, Leary was dismissed
from Harvard for these activities, but his mission did not
end. He founded a private research group called the International Foundation for Internal Freedom (IFIF), and set up
a psychedelic study center in a 64-room mansion on a
4,000-acre estate in Millbrook, New York, donated by one
of his followers, multi-millionaire William Hitchcock, heir
to the Gulf Oil fortune. Leary garnered the attention of mid-

dle America when he began to use the media to preach his psychedelic message: "Turn on. Tune in. Drop out."

In California, author Ken Kesey took his first LSD trip in 1960 with the blessings of the United States government as a volunteer at the Menlo Park veterans' hospital drug experiment. It was Kesey who first called LSD "acid." And much to the dismay of researchers like Leary, who gave his followers LSD under controlled conditions, Kesey doled out acid in "electric" Kool-Aid.

Kesey's growing band of followers, known as "Merry Pranksters," according to the Sterns, were

> an entourage of proto-hippies energized by fantastic acid visions. [They] traveled in the original psychedelic bus . . . painted in the wildest shades of schizophrenichrome. They wore superhero capes and goggles and American flags and glow-in-the-dark, on-the-warpath uniforms. They declared themselves living works of art.[11]

In 1965, LSD was still legal, and Kesey began to hold "acid tests" where acid was given to thousands at huge parties where people decorated their bodies with Day-Glo paint, watched protoplasmic light shows, and danced all night long to the psychedelic rock of the Grateful Dead. Kesey's acid tests spread LSD use far and wide and the psychedelic revolution quickly overtook America. The result is described by the Sterns:

> Hordes of vaguely disenchanted, vaguely antiwar and antiestablishment sixties people were encouraged by these acid tests to drop out and embark on the great grope towards a mental condition they called expanded consciousness. By early 1966, the center of the hippie universe was between 1400 and 1800 Haight Street, [in the Haight-Ashbury neighborhood] where most of San Francisco's acidheads were encamped—and hundreds more were arriving every week from around the nation. They slept on the sidewalk and in doorways. They sat together playing guitars and tambourines and flutes. They sold beads and buttons and panhandled spare change and copped and sold marijuana joints and acid tabs. Hell's Angels hung out in front of Tracy's Doughnut Shop; acidheads made love in the meditation room at the back of the Psychedelic Shop. . . .

Before they emerged as a provocative public issue, the random congress of ex-beatniks, disenchanted lefties, folk rockers, street people, and dropouts had begun to see themselves as a new tribe. Throughout 1966, after the Trips Festival in January, the hippies' growing sense of community was expressed in street fairs, a summer-solstice festival, acid-rock concerts, a "Love Pageant Rally" in October (called to mark the sixth of the month, the day California's law making LSD illegal went into effect), and climactically, the Human Be-In of January 1967. The lofty promise of the Be-In . . . was to . . . powwow, celebrate, and prophesy the epoch of liberation, love, peace, compassion, and unity of mankind.[12]

By July 1967, the "Summer of Love" was in full swing, and hippie neighborhoods modeled on Haight-Ashbury began to pop up in every major American city. The media jumped on the hippie bandwagon and scarcely a week went by when some major magazine like *Time, Newsweek,* or *Life* did not have a story on some aspect of the hippie revolution. While the war raged in Vietnam, America's children danced and sang and put flowers in their hair.

1968: The Year of Chaos

It seemed that all of the problems of the sixties—the Vietnam War, civil rights, the counterculture, anti-war protests, and national politics—came to a fiery head in 1968 in a series of events that left many Americans wondering if their country would not disintegrate into anarchy.

In January, 80,000 North Vietnamese coordinated a massive attack known as the "Tet Offensive," driving American troops out of 100 major positions in the South. This huge loss was a major political turning point in the United States. President Johnson's guarantees of an American victory began to ring hollow. Polls showed for the first time that a majority of Americans disapproved of Johnson's handling of the war. Every day protesters would gather around the White House and chant "Hey, hey LBJ, how many kids did you kill today?" Seeing no way out, the president announced on March 31 that he would not run for a second term.

Several days earlier, Martin Luther King Jr. had journeyed

to Memphis, Tennessee, to support that city's striking garbage workers. While King led a peaceful protest, black teenagers began smashing store windows and looting. King called off the march, but returned to the city on April 3 to address supporters. The next day, King was assassinated while standing on the balcony of his hotel room. When news of King's death was announced, riots exploded in black neighborhoods in dozens of major American cities. The evening news showed army troops in tanks and jeeps spraying tear gas and wielding truncheons in Chicago, Detroit, Newark, Cleveland, Los Angeles and elsewhere. In Washington, D.C., the riots spread to within two blocks of the White House. As fully armed army troops arrived in personnel carriers to restore order, to many Americans, the United States was beginning to look like Vietnam.

After the riots were quelled, Johnson's decision not to run opened the field up for several presidential candidates. Vice president Hubert Humphrey ran with the pledge to continue Johnson's policies in Vietnam. Wisconsin senator Eugene

Martin Luther King Jr. addresses his followers after cancelling a march in Alabama. The next day, King was assassinated, an event that grieved the nation and caused several black riots.

McCarthy ran on a platform of immediate withdrawal from Indochina. And JFK's brother, Robert Kennedy, also ran on a liberal platform of peace in Vietnam and many new social programs to aid blacks at home.

Bobby Kennedy, like his brother, was rich, handsome, and charismatic. He seemed the most likely to win the election in November. Then, after winning the Democratic primary in California on June 4, Kennedy was shot and killed in Los Angeles.

With Kennedy gone, Humphrey, who had the support of Johnson and the Democratic leadership, seemed like the man who would run for president in November. With the probable nomination of someone who supported the war, tens of thousands of protesters decided to travel to the Democratic Convention held in Chicago between August 26 and 29. The group included a diverse range of peace groups and a new brand of brash protesters—the Yippies—who sought direct confrontation with Chicago police.

Chicago mayor Richard J. Daley denied permits to demonstrate or camp in the city's parks to the protesters. He also called in 12,000 police, 5,000 national guard, and 7,500 army troops. On the night of August 28, around 3,000 protesters attempted to enter the convention hall where delegates were debating Vietnam policy. Police began to beat, gas, and arrest anyone they could get hold of, including reporters, convention delegates, and even innocent bystanders. As Americans watched the streets of Chicago fill with blood and tear gas, hopes for a Democratic presidential victory dimmed.

The earth-shattering events of 1968—the Tet Offensive, assassinations, riots, and more—ended when Republican Richard Nixon won the election in November. Under Nixon, the war in Vietnam continued for another five years.

Radicalized Americans

After the violence in Chicago and riots in black neighborhoods, many Americans became extremely radicalized against their government. The peaceful protests and sit-ins of the early sixties had turned into an all-out war against authorities. Nowhere was this more obvious than in black ghettos across America where calls for black equality had turned into cries of "Black Power!"

The Black Power movement was led by a group known as the Black Panthers, an organization founded by Bobby Seale and Huey Newton. The Panthers, like the hippies, grew out of the neighborhoods of the San Francisco Bay area. Unlike the hippies, however, the Panthers were raised in the mean streets of East Oakland, where the white police force kept the black neighborhoods under tight militaristic control.

The Panthers expressed their outrage in a stylish paramilitary pose that was quickly imitated by many in the counterculture—both black and white. The symbol of the Panthers was a raised clenched fist, and they wore black berets, black leather jackets, and carried carbines, striking fear and wonder into anyone who saw them. Eldridge Cleaver, whose prison writings inspired the movement, described the first time he saw the Panthers:

> I spun around in my seat and saw the most beautiful sight I had ever seen: four black men wearing black berets, powder blue shirts, black leather jackets, black trousers, shiny black shoes—and each with a gun! In front was Huey P. Newton with a riot pump shotgun in his right hand, barrel pointed down to the floor. Beside him was Bobby Seale, the handle of a .45 caliber automatic showing from its holster on his right hip, just below the hem of his jacket. A few steps behind Seale was Bobby Hutton, the barrel of his shotgun at his feet. Next to him was Sherwin Forte, an M1 carbine with a banana clip cradled in his arms. . . . Every eye in the room was riveted upon them. . . . Where was my mind at? Blown![13]

The Black Panthers were extremely radical, even going so far as to advocate the assassination of Nixon. But they had more to their program than violence. The Panthers instituted programs to give free breakfasts to children in the ghetto and opened free clinics in many neighborhoods. And their message was popular—by 1969 there were Black Panther chapters in thirty-seven cities.

The police and FBI began to take direct action against the Black Panthers. In 1969, a series of middle-of-the-night raids in Los Angeles and Chicago killed two Panther leaders and wounded seven. By the mid-seventies, more than a hundred Panthers were in jail and four hundred were under indictment. Dozens more had been killed in shootouts with police.

The Dream Is Over

When the Beatles broke up in 1970, to many it was more than the death of a band—it also seemed like the end of a dream. While the Beatles sang "All You Need is Love" during the Summer of Love, on his first solo album, John Lennon sang "the dream is over." A movement based on the slogan, "Do your own thing," could not sustain itself over a long period of time.

The Woodstock Arts and Crafts Festival in upstate New York in August 1969 had shown that half a million people could assemble, take drugs, and peacefully listen to rock and roll for three days. But in December at the West Coast version of Woodstock in Altamont, California, acid-crazed bikers called Hell's Angels mercilessly beat hippies who were assembled to hear the Rolling Stones perform. A black man was stabbed to death, putting a sad finish to a colorful decade.

Hard drugs and hard times had infiltrated into the hippie neighborhoods, driving many flower children out of the cities and onto rural communes where they tried to construct utopias in the forests. Strung-out junkies and prostitutes took their place. The shining lights of the sixties music scene—Janis Joplin, Jimi Hendrix, Jim Morrison—flickered out one by one—dead from drug overdoses.

In January 1973, Nixon declared "peace with honor" in Vietnam and the United States ended its formal participation in the war. The South quickly fell to the Communists. During the war almost 3.4 million Americans had served in Vietnam; 58,183 were killed, 303,713 were wounded. Countless others carried the emotional scars of the war with them for years—a study conducted in the 1980s showed that over one-third of the homeless in America were veterans of the war. In addition to the American casualties, over three million Vietnamese on both sides were killed and countless others wounded.

Without resistance to the war to hold them together, the counterculture began to drift. But other causes founded in the sixties gained popularity. On April 22, 1970, the first Earth Day was held in Washington where more than 10,000 people gathered to talk about air and water pollution. The growing concern over the environment prompted Nixon to create the Environmental Protection Agency that year. Other laws such as the Clean Air and Clean Water Acts grew out of these new environmental concerns.

The growing women's liberation movement also began to gain ground in the early seventies. When the feminist magazine *Ms.* published its first issue in 1972, all 250,000 copies sold out in eight days. Dozens of women wrote books about the inequality between men and women, and words such as "sexism," "feminism," and "male chauvinism" entered the American lexicon.

Many lesbians were attracted to the women's movement, and their struggle became part of a larger struggle for gay rights, which also grew out of sixties civil rights protests. In 1970, gay and lesbian activists began asking for an end to legal discrimination and oppression. In big cities such as New York and San Francisco, homosexuals began to open bars and shops without the fear of police harassment for the first time. By 1973, there were nearly 800 organizations fighting for gay rights both locally and nationally.

In the mid-1970s, America's economic security was rocked when gasoline prices doubled in a matter of months. People started buying Japanese compact cars and America's steel and auto industries instituted a series of massive layoffs. The American Dream of the fifties and sixties was replaced for millions with recessions, layoffs, and unemployment. It no longer seemed to make sense for college students to attend rallies and sit-ins instead of classes.

Counterculture to Mainstream Culture

The views expressed by the leading voices of the counterculture were extremely controversial in the sixties and have remained so since that time. Millions of today's Americans are of the belief that the world would have been a better place if the years of "free love," LSD, and protest had never happened. Others think that saying "no" to war, expanding human consciousness with drugs, and relaxing the rigid social mores of the fifties were worth the costs.

Whatever one's belief about that time so long ago, the fact remains that the fallout—good and bad—from the sixties counterculture remains a part of mainstream culture today. And it is intricately woven into the social fabric of America at the dawn of the twenty-first century.

Notes

1. David Farber, *The Age of Great Dreams: America in the 1960s.* New York: Hill and Wang,1994, pp. 8–9.
2. Quoted in Douglas T. Miller & Marion Nowak, *The Fifties: The Way We Really Were.* Garden City, NY: Doubleday & Co., 1975, p. 365.
3. Tom Hayden, *Reunion: A Memoir.* New York: Random House, 1988, pp. 31–32.
4. Quoted in the Editors of Time-Life Books, *Turbulent Years: The 60s.* Alexandria, VA: Time-Life Books, 1998, p. 154.
5. Quoted in Jann Wenner, ed., *20 Years of* Rolling Stone: *What a Long, Strange Trip It's Been.* New York: Straight Arrow Publishers, 1987, p. 37.
6. Farber, *The Age of Great Dreams,* p. 129.
7. Quoted in Farber, *The Age of Great Dreams,* p. 134.
8. Richard Stacewicz, *Winter Soldiers: An Oral History of Vietnam Veterans Against the War.* New York: Twayne Publishers, 1997, p. 85.
9. Jane and Michael Stern, *Sixties People.* New York: Alfred A. Knopf, 1990, pp. 148–49.
10. Timothy Leary, *The Politics of Ecstasy.* Berkeley, CA: Ronin Publishing, 1998, p. 118.
11. Stern, *Sixties People,* p. 150.
12. Stern, *Sixties People,* p. 152.
13. Quoted in Stern, *Sixties People,* p. 191.

Chapter 1

Seeds of the Counterculture: The Early 60s

Chapter Preface

The Constitution of the United States guarantees free speech and the right of the people to assemble peaceably and to petition the government for redress of grievances. In the 1950s, however, few Americans alive had ever seen any sort of massive outpouring of protest against government policy.

The people who ran the government, schools, police departments, and other institutions were raised during the massive poverty of the Great Depression and had fought side by side during World War II. To be sure, there were labor marches and rallies during the depression, but when the war came, millions of people complied with their government's orders, obediently joined the army, and fought a common enemy. The lives of those who remained in America during the war were rigidly controlled by government-ordered civil defense drills and the rationing of food, clothing, and gasoline.

Baby boomers had no such memory, though. They grew up in a decade that belonged to the young, where their every whim and desire was indulged. Parents who had suffered during the Great Depression did not want their children to know such deprivation. In *Loose Change,* author Sara Davidson explains how this situation affected the baby boom generation:

> [We] thought life was free and would never run out. There were good people and bad people and we could tell them apart by a look or by words spoken in code. We were certain that we belonged to a generation that was special. We did not need or care about history because we had sprung from nowhere. We said what we thought and demanded what was right because there was no opposition.

It was in this sort of atmosphere that the early rumblings of protest began in a decade that would be rife with angry mobs, tear gas, broken windows, overturned cars, and people being beaten by the police. When the first demonstrators peacefully assembled in the early sixties, however, few could foresee what their small movement would become. By the 1970s, the demonstrators and their supporters would grow into a movement that encompassed millions.

The Free Speech Movement in Berkeley

David Lance Goines

The first massive campus revolt of the 1960s began in late 1964 at the University of California at Berkeley. At the time, several civil rights and other political groups had been setting up tables near the college entrance in order to raise money and pass out leaflets. The protests began in the autumn of 1964 when the school's Board of Regents told students that they could no longer use that space because they were blocking pedestrian traffic. Students believed that the real reason was that the conservative Board of Regents did not appreciate their left-leaning activities.

When told of the new rules the groups banded together and formed the Free Speech Movement (FSM). The FSM protested by continuing to hand out leaflets in front of the college. When activist Jack Weinberg was arrested by the Berkeley police and put in a squad car, hundreds of demonstrators surrounded the car for over twenty-four hours. Thousands more gathered on Sproul Plaza to protest. The demonstration ended peacefully but the battle lines were drawn.

After months of negotiations with the Board of Regents—and the suspension of dozens of students who violated the rules—the FSM organized a sit-in at the administration offices in Sproul Hall after a speech by activist Mario Savio. About 1,500 students took over the building and 800 were arrested. Although this was the first major student takeover of campus offices, it was not the last. The practice spread to dozens of other campuses before the sixties drew to a close.

Excerpted from David Lance Goines, *The Free Speech Movement: Coming of Age in the 1960's*. Reprinted with permission from Ten Speed Press, Berkeley, CA. Copyright ©1993 by David Lance Goines. Available from your local bookseller, by calling Ten Speed Press at 800-841-2665, or by visiting us online at www.tenspeed.com.

> In the following selection, artist and author David Goines
> relates his personal recollection of the sit-in at Sproul Hall.
> The narrative is joined by Sue Stein, Kate Coleman, Bob
> Starobin, Sam Slatkin, and Ron Anastasi who were also part
> of the sit-in at Sproul Hall in 1964.

On December 2, following a huge noon rally in Sproul
Plaza, about fifteen hundred people packed all four
floors of Sproul Hall. A young student was at the door of
Sproul Hall right after [activist] Mario [Savio] had finished
his speech, standing in a truculent posture with balled fists,
as though to defend the doors against all these Communists.
As the waves of students approached and passed him, he
looked astonished, put down his hands and walked away.

Charlie Powell urged the crowd to disperse, but was
booed by the demonstrators. Mario said that he was "not
only a strikebreaker, but a fink." Throughout the afternoon,
students ambled in and out at will, and the initially tightly
packed mass declined to a more comfortable number. . . .

Rope Bridges

Just before seven in the evening, University police told us
that the building would be closed, and that anyone who
wanted to leave could do so, but no one could enter. At this
point, the cops discovered that they couldn't lock the doors,
and as pairs of policemen guarded each entrance, locksmiths
were brought in to do what they could.

Ropes dangled from the second-floor balcony, and food
and a few demonstrators were hauled into the building. A
line was passed across the plaza between the Student Union
and Sproul Hall, and baskets of food and messages went
along it from the Student Union to the eight or nine hundred
remaining demonstrators. . . .

Steve Weissman claimed that in Peace Corps training he'd
learned to make rope bridges, and that we should send out
for the equipment to make a bridge between Sproul Hall and
the Student Union building. Steve's plan for building a rope

bridge had been discussed in the Steering Committee meeting and we voted against it. . . . We had people who were ready, willing and able to do it, but we felt that it would be just too risky, and if someone were hurt or killed on it, it would be really disastrous for us.

The floors were divided up for various activities: first floor was for sleeping, second floor was wide open for anything anybody wanted to do, third floor was study hall and fourth floor was study and sleeping area. Every floor had monitors on it in proportion to the number of people, and members of the Steering Committee made themselves highly visible, talking with people and entering into impromptu discussions.

After movies (two comedies: a Laurel and Hardy film and *Operation Abolition*), Chanukah services, dancing and speeches, people settled down for the night, either to sleep or to study. Jeff Lustig and Lee Glickman played a giant game of chess on the linoleum-tile squares, using coke bottles for pawns and playing cards for the other pieces. Informal classes were held in corners and under stairwells. Hand-drawn posters advertised "Free University of California" courses.

At about four in the afternoon, I had seen [police] Lieutenant Chandler going up to a bathroom door on the third floor at the far end. He had keys in his hand and it looked to me like he was going to start locking bathroom doors. I got between him and the door, and told him that if he locked the door we'd piss in the hall; we'd sector off a part of the building as a latrine and God damn it we'd piss in it. He got very shaken up and took off. He was the easiest guy to intimidate that I knew of; you'd just yell at him and he'd fall apart. We were afraid that someone else would try to lock the doors to the bathrooms, so I told several monitors to take the doors off their hinges or jam the locks. When we heard that the police were coming, we put some of the doors back on their hinges. . . .

Breaking into Offices

As the evening wore on, the possibility of arrest seemed to lessen; and at midnight we heard from Mrs. Kerr [the wife of Board of Regents President Clark Kerr] that there would be no arrests. Joan Baez, who had sung our generation's anthem, "The Times They Are A-Changin'," during the rally and walked into the building leading us in "We Shall Overcome," left—though not before companionably sharing peanut butter sandwiches with the students.

During the sixties, demonstrators used sit-ins as a form of protest. Here, students form a sit-in at the Washington Monument in Washington, D.C.

During the sit-in a campus policeman peered into President Emeritus Gordon Sproul's office, and seeing papers strewn about reported that the demonstrators had broken in. This was not true, and the report was later shown to be in error, as Sproul was a notoriously untidy man (his secretary later confessed, "We kept a messy office"), but it led the assistant county prosecutor—Edwin Meese III—who was sitting in the campus police headquarters in the Sproul Hall basement, to call the governor and tell him, "They're busting up the place. We have to go in." [Governor Edmund G.] Brown then issued orders to arrest us, and [Chancellor E.W.] Strong, who had been closeted in University Hall with [Clark] Kerr all evening, was elected to give us the news. This was not what Kerr had wanted. Kerr had decided to ignore the sit-in for as long as he could, figuring that the initial excitement would die down, the majority of the students would lose interest and become disenchanted with the demonstration, and the numbers that he would have to deal with would dwindle to a few hard-core activists. In this, as in other matters, he was frustrated by agendas beyond his control.

Though strictly speaking we had not broken into Sproul's office, we had indeed broken in elsewhere:

[Activist] *Kate Coleman* [remembers]: During the Sproul Hall sit-in we actually did break into some of the offices. There we found stuff on the University's contracts with A.P. Giannini's Bank of America, agribusiness and federal weapons research. All along, the administration had been going on about "off-campus" influence on the FSM, but it paled beside the "off-campus" influence on UC that we discovered there. We felt totally vindicated. This was a big step in my own radicalization; after others had gotten into the offices and were rifling through files, I came in and looked too. The room I was in was on the east side of the building and was full of filing cabinets. It was a big thing for me to be prowling around where I didn't belong, finding out things that had been hidden. I think that's what got me into investigative journalism: if you do only what you're allowed to do, and ask questions only where you're supposed to ask them, you never find out the truth.

Five Minutes to Clear Out

At twelve-thirty everything was quiet, and I went down to the first floor and conked out on a sleeping bag. At about a quarter of two a newsman's lights woke me up, and shortly afterward I heard that police were on their way. Suzanne Goldberg and I were appointed fourth-floor monitor captains. We held two practice "pack-ins" like the one that we'd had around the dean's offices on October 1, got fire extinguishers ready to douse tear-gas bombs, and stacked everything that might hurt if you got dragged over it in a glassed-off section near the main door.

At 3:00 AM, Chancellor Strong announced that we were to leave or face disciplinary action:

May I have your attention? I am Dr. Edward Strong, chancellor of the Berkeley campus. I have an announcement.

This assemblage has developed to such a point that the purpose and work of the University have been materially impaired. (*Loud cheers and applause.*) It is clear that there have been acts of disobedience and illegality which cannot be tolerated in a responsible educational center and would not be tolerated anywhere in our society.

The University has shown great restraint and patience in exercising its legitimate authority in order to allow every opportunity for expressing differing points of view. The University always stands ready to engage in the established and accepted procedures for resolving differences of opinion.

I request that each of you cease your participation in this unlawful assembly.

I urge you, both individually and collectively, to leave this area. I request that you immediately disperse. Failure to disperse will result in disciplinary action by the University.

Please go.

The elevators had been turned off around seven o'clock, and we'd taken all the standing ashtrays and green metal wastebaskets and put them in front of the elevator doors to act as a warning of sorts in case some sort of surprise got past the sentries. When Strong came out of the elevator on the fourth floor, he didn't see them, and kicked them over with a big operatic crash. It startled him, and made him even angrier, and instead of saying "Please go," he spat, "Now go! *Git!*" as though we were animals. We were shocked by the venom in his voice. I was standing behind him and beside Lieutenant Chandler, and when Strong finished his announcement, I moved to the back of the corridor and Suzanne to the front.

Lieutenant Chandler succeeded Strong, announced that we were in violation of the law and gave us five minutes to clear out. Nobody went.

Forty-five minutes later, Governor Brown announced that he had directed the California Highway Patrol and the

Alameda County Sheriff's Department to arrest the demonstrators. As though awaiting his signal, the elevator doors opened, policemen came out and the arrests began. . . .

Command Central

Bob Starobin [recalls]: Command Central was set up by Marty Roysher in an apartment behind Wells Fargo Bank; they had two phones and a walkie-talkie and were in communication with Sproul Hall, which was right over the roof.

I was at Command Central until one-thirty, and then went home. Everyone thought that there weren't going to be any arrests until the next day. At Command Central, we were sending out kids on motor scooters to all the police stations to see if there was any activity, and there was nothing. Every half hour, a guy would come back with a report. All of a sudden, around a quarter of two, they started up. We knew that the police were coming almost an hour before they arrived at Sproul. Then I got a call about four-thirty—they were arresting people.

Sam Slatkin: Some plainclothes high-up official pointed at [protester] Jack Weinberg, and two or three Oakland or Alameda sheriffs went after him. Jack tried to get out of their reach—he was standing in between the balcony windows and one of the tables and looking the other way—and he didn't get very far before they got him. They tried to pull a similar thing with Weissman, but we opened up a passageway for him and closed it after him and he got out the window.

There were two charges, one was to get Jack and one to get the microphone. When they did get the microphone it was replaced—one that somebody happened to have, it wasn't very good but it did the job—and they didn't get that one again.

Ron Anastasi: Jack was arrested early Thursday morning in the sudden police raid on the microphone. After we got the microphone back in working order, we decided to pack in around it to prevent another successful raid. Everyone was very upset by that first raid. Jo Freeman was screaming, "Link arms! Link arms!" and I had to pull rank on her, saying, "It is a Steering Committee decision not to link arms." Then several of the Steering Committee members decided that Steve Weissman should stay on campus and

direct the strike. Steve really protested, but finally we all agreed
that he should go out and direct the strike, and we set up a rope
from the window, and if the police came Steve was to go down the
rope. We had realized that we had too much leadership inside and
not enough outside. When Steve left, he was about two feet ahead
of the cops. They were hopping over people behind him. . . .

Battling Police

Immediately after the building was closed, at seven, we'd
started having communication problems. Walkie-talkies had
been rented for $5 the first day and $2.50 the second day. My
girlfriend Sally picked them up in San Francisco. Andy Wells
had one inside, and some random person had one on the outside, and we weren't getting the information we needed. So
we decided that a Steering Committee member should go
outside, and sent Marty Roysher. He really didn't want to.
No one wanted to leave. We argued about who should go out,
and Marty was the worst arguer, so he had to go.

We got a report that the police were going to use tear gas,
and Mike Smith, who'd had experience with tear gas, said
that it was heavy and sinks. Because of that, we decided to
move people to the upper floors. Tear gas used in confined
spaces could be toxic or cause panic. He suggested that the
only thing to do would be to use wet handkerchiefs over our
noses and mouths. It wouldn't be much, but it would be better than nothing. So members of the Steering Committee
went to the different floors with pitchers of water. I was going up and down the aisles pouring water on handkerchiefs
and scarves that people were holding up, some of the girls
were sitting there holding up embroidered handkerchiefs
and kerchiefs, and these kids were just shaking, and I was
shaking, we were all so scared. And yet, they were staying
there and doing it. That was the most profound moment. I
really felt an incredible oneness with everyone; we are not
going to give in.

We'd decided that people would grab the tear-gas cylin-
ders and throw them out the windows. People from CORE
[Congress for Racial Equality]—people who had been ar-

rested before—were supposed to be on each floor, to keep things under control if the police showed up.

During the second attack on the microphone, I was standing on top of the card file. A policeman was hitting people, and when the panic and noise level were at a peak, all of a sudden an American flag came shooting through the air and hit the guy, and he picked it up, and it looked like he didn't believe it somehow. Myself and Hilbert [Coleman] grabbed the end of the staff and started a tug-of-war between ourselves and the police officer, and we finally got it back and handed it back to the guy who had thrown it. It seemed very symbolic.

Thursday morning at about eight o'clock, I got a call from Command Central that twenty cars were on their way to park in around the police cars and that a phone chain had formed to get more cars. And I said, "What? Tell them to stop that right now!" The action had already been initiated, and the cars were on their way. Can you imagine what would have happened then? People would have sat down around their cars. . . . There would have been a full-scale war. Jesus.

Arrests Begin

The arrests began on our floor, and Suzanne and I led singing and did our best to keep up morale. As the cops ground along, methodically busting everyone in their path. . . .

When the police got within a few rows of me, I sat down—I'd been on my feet to make my voice carry better, and to keep a high profile for the crowd. [Police Sergeant] Glenn and three others held a tête-à-tête and skipped over the people in front to get at me. Though it was 5:06 AM, I was only the forty-third person to be arrested; the police had a long day ahead of them.

I went limp and was carried by two cops, one of whom bent my left arm sharply behind me, while the other put a "come-along" hold on my right wrist; the net result was that I was completely off the ground for most of the trip. Although it hurt a lot, as indeed it was meant to, I managed to keep relatively silent and made the front page of the morn-

ing *Oakland Tribune* with my mouth shut. A full-face photo was captioned "Tight-Lipped Demonstrator." My brothers and sisters were simultaneously horrified and thrilled,
proud of their big brother's notoriety and ashamed of his being hauled off to jail on the front page of the newspaper. My
parents were aggressively defensive, and publicly pro-
claimed that they were proud of me for standing up for my
principles. My mother has a scrapbook of every newspaper
or magazine account and photo of me.

Tossed into the elevator, where I landed on a fellow
demonstrator, I broke my vow of silence and called Sergeant
Glenn a son of a bitch. Accompanied by a policeman, the
five or six of us rode down to the basement for preliminary
booking. One of the guys made like the cop was an elevator
boy, asking, "Mezzanine, please." We thought that was rich.
We were fingerprinted and photographed, and when we
were questioned amused ourselves by deviling the booking
officers. When they asked "race," I replied "human," instead
of Caucasian or Negro or whatever they obviously wanted.
Everyone who heard me followed suit, to the ill-concealed
annoyance of the already bone-tired cops. Just as dawn
broke we were ushered into a waiting Alameda County
Sheriff's bus for a ride to Santa Rita county jail.

The police had decided to let gravity do some of the work
and began arresting demonstrators from the fourth floor
down. The relatively small population of the fourth floor
was entirely in custody before the third floor got any attention at all. They'd only arrested some of the students on the
third floor before they switched to the second floor, where
demonstrators had moved from both the first and third floors
to form a massive people-jam. Police spent most of the day
clearing the second floor. Men were taken directly to the
small campus police station in the basement, fingerprinted
and searched. Women were taken first to the dean of students' office, searched by a police matron, and then taken to
the basement for fingerprinting. Though any demonstrator
was free to go at any time before arrest, I do not believe that
many left; indeed, quite a few climbed into the building dur-

ing the day in order to participate. In all, the arrests of some eight hundred students, University employees and former students took almost as many policemen thirteen hours. As the jails filled up, amazed rummies and short-timers found themselves awakened and unceremoniously cut loose. Berkeley, Oakland and Santa Rita jails overflowed, and a loosely guarded group ended up in the National Guard Armory in San Leandro. This, the largest mass arrest in California history, got headlines all over the world, even, to our delight, in Uganda.

White Students Join Fight for Black Rights

Sara Davidson

In 1960, the centuries-old discrimination against African Americans by white society continued unabated in most regions of the country in spite of antisegregation laws that were passed in the 1950s. In the Deep South, black people could not use the same rest room, drink from the same water fountain, or eat at the same lunch counter as whites. In California, blacks were denied decent jobs, quality housing, and other necessities. Black groups such as the Congress of Racial Equality (CORE), which was founded in 1942 to combat discrimination, organized sit-ins and protests and slowly broke down the barriers of segregation. They were joined, in many cases, by middle-class white college students who put their beliefs into action in order to help the African American cause.

Sara Davidson was one such student who detailed her political awakening in the early sixties when she was a student at the University of California at Berkeley. Davidson is a graduate of the Columbia School of Journalism who has written for magazines such as *Harpers, The Atlantic, Ramparts, Rolling Stone, Ms.,* and others.

I n the early spring Negroes appeared on the campus. There was a demonstration going on at the Lucky Market on Telegraph. CORE [Congress of Racial Equality] had declared war on all Lucky Markets for failing to recruit and

Excerpted from Sara Davidson, *Loose Change: Three Women of the Sixties.* Reprinted with permission from the author.

train Negroes for good jobs. After a week of picketing, the demonstrators had invented a new tactic: a shop-in. This is how it worked: students would wheel shopping carts down the aisles, load them to the brim and abandon them at the check stand saying coyly, "Oh, I forgot my wallet." Others went around rearranging the shelves and dropping food on the floor.

By the third day of the shop-in, the store was a shambles. Broken eggs, rotting vegetables and smashed loaves of bread were piled four feet high on the check stands. When I walked past the market with [my friend] Tasha, I felt sick. Tasha was angry. "Those kids are acting like animals. It's disgusting."

A friend of ours who was a law student said he was organizing a group to help clean up the market, "I'm not against CORE, but their tactics are absolutely contrary to the law. It gives CORE a bad image."

One of the demonstrators brayed, "We're not interested in our public image. We're interested in stopping business for a discriminatory employer."

I said I was going in for some tomatoes. Trying to look blasé, I picked my way through the wreckage but as I was clearing the check stand, I spotted [my friend] Susie, who was throwing potatoes on the floor and shot me a look of such patronizing scorn that I felt exposed.

The truth was—and this was a secret I had told no mortal . . . —I didn't like Negroes. At my high school, half the student body were Negroes, which meant that my friends and I could not go to the bathroom alone or dawdle in the halls without asking for trouble: knife fights, hair pulling, cigarette burnings, who knew. . . .

Do You Know What It's Like?

We had never mixed socially in high school so I was not happy when the door opened at a party in Berkeley and a contingent of Negroes cruised in. I remember feeling especially pretty that night, wearing a lavender spring dress, my hair up and a pair of amethyst earrings from my grandmother. A tall Negro named OB asked me to dance. I refused. A song from the brand-new "Meet the Beatles" album was playing. When the Beatles sang, "I'll Never Dance with Another," all the kids threw back their heads and wailed, "Wooooo!" But OB stood apart. The pupils of his eyes were so small that it looked as if he had no pupils, just two flat brown disks. "Do you know what it's like?" he said.

"What what's like?"

He did not move. "Like, bein' a spade." The flatness of his eyes was unnerving me. "I can't get no job. I can't go to school. I can't live in a decent house."

When a slow number came on OB put his arms around me. Over his shoulder I saw [my friend] Candy beaming approval. My body went rigid and it was not until the dance was over and OB was gone that I wondered if he was right, maybe I didn't know what it was like at all.

Getting a Political Education

My political education began at the feet of OB and other street hustlers from East Oakland. We would meet on the steps of the Student Union and they would talk about going hungry in the slums and seeing their sisters turn tricks and their brothers shoot junk. I remember how it felt to hear, for the first time, how unfair it was. Something had to be done.

By the time I learned about the demonstration to be held at the Sheraton Palace in San Francisco, I was ready to go. Everyone was going. The demonstration would be the biggest social event of the semester.

The Sheraton Palace was one of the great old hotels; it covered an entire block and employed 550 people, but only 31 Negroes. An Ad Hoc Committee was asking the hotel to sign a no-bias hiring pact. The hotel was refusing, so a massive demonstration had been called for Friday, March 6, at 6 P.M.

It was 8 P.M. when I drove across the Bay Bridge with Tasha, Steven Silver, Candy and four others in Tasha's red convertible. We had decided to dress nicely, the boys wearing suits and the girls in dresses, so people could identify with our cause and not be alienated by a beatnik atmosphere. Because of the traffic we had to park a mile away. As we walked hurriedly, we began to hear roaring, like the muffled cheering that erupts from a distant sports arena.

> What do we want?
> Freedom!
> When?
> Now!

We rounded the comer. I had never seen anything like it! An army of kids, two thousand or more, was circling around and around the Palace. The night gleamed with lights. Policemen rode horses. There were three picket lines on three sides of the Palace, each line sending its chants into the air.

We joined one line and I was handed a sign, "Jim Crow Must Go." What does that mean? I asked Candy. She wasn't sure. Her sign said, "Tokenism Is Not Enough." I waved to my friends and gossiped and sang as loud as I could, "We Shall Overcome." After I had checked out all the faces in the line, I grabbed Candy's arm, we ran around the comer and joined the next picket line.

"You guys, isn't this astounding!" We turned and saw Susie.

"Where's Jeff?"

She motioned with her head. Jeff was a monitor, directing the line; he wore a white arm band over his jacket.

Moving Inside

At 10 P.M. one of the monitors announced over a bullhorn that we were moving inside. There was a court injunction barring us from entering the hotel. I looked at the policemen reining in their skittish horses and said to Susie, "I'm scared." She whispered, "So am I."

"Okay," yelled the monitor, "Pair up, a guy and a girl, and let's go, but keep it quiet, no singing, shhhh!"

Jeff appeared and took Susie. A strange boy linked his arm through mine and another took Candy's arm. We formed a double line and shuffled up the steps and through the doors into the lobby. Tourists backed away before us. We sat down, a thousand shiny-faced students, on the red Chinese rugs among potted palms. We looked at each other, not knowing what was coming. It grew hot, we took off sweaters. I was becoming very nervous. I didn't want to go to jail. I didn't want my future ruined. What would my parents think? Every few minutes a troublemaker in our ranks would stand and cry out, "Time to escalate!"

"Shhhh! Keep it down."

I kept plotting my escape. OB would say I was chicken but I didn't care. At two in the morning, a Negro girl, Tracy Sims, stood on a marble table and shouted, "Okay. The hotel has broken faith. Are you ready to go to jail for what you believe?"

"Yes!" the crowd roared, but Candy and I looked at each other and mouthed, "No." On the pretext of having to go to the bathroom, we walked through the lobby and straight out the door.

From the sidewalk, we watched as demonstrators started blocking the hotel doors, inviting arrest. "Pack in and lock arms, hold on!" They went limp and sang "We Shall Not Be Moved." (Where did they learn all this? I wondered.) After more than a hundred had been carried into paddy wagons, the leaders decided bail money had run out and the demonstration should continue legally.

We Were Committed

Students poured out of the hotel and we all continued circling. I spotted Susie and Jeff, they hadn't gone to jail! The sun came up. Saturday shoppers appeared on Market Street and I could see from their startled mouths, they had no idea what to make of us. How proud I felt. I belonged to a great new body of students who cared about the problems of the world. No longer would youth be apathetic. That was the fifties. We were *committed*.

I had taken six food breaks and was heading for the car and a nap when, at two the following afternoon, Tracy Sims jumped on a speaker van and shouted: "We won! The hotel has signed a no-bias hiring pact. Let me hear you. What do we want?"

In the din that followed, Candy began to cry. Susie looked dazed. Jeff clasped his hands and shook them above his head like a boxing champ. I laughed and screamed with my last stores of energy:

"Freedom!"

Feminist Stirrings in the Early Sixties

Betty Friedan

While millions of women spent the sixties supporting civil
rights for African Americans and protesting against the war in
Vietnam, there was still inequality between the sexes in
movements dominated by men. After the protests, the
marches, and the sit-ins, women were still assigned the age-
old tasks of cooking, childcare, and office work. The feminist
movement, while not widely popular until the 1970s, was
formed in the bedrock principles of equality and individual
rights that were forged in the sixties.

One of the earliest and most well-known voices calling
for equal rights for women was Betty Friedan. In 1957,
Friedan took a survey of her former classmates of the Smith
College class of 1942 and found a profound unhappiness
with many of the responses. In 1963, she published her find-
ings in the groundbreaking *Feminine Mystique* which
warned that millions of women were losing their own personal identity by seeking fulfillment through their homes,
husbands, and family, which she said was creating a
depressed, neurotic generation of women. Friedan carried
her message to college campuses in speeches such as this
one given at the University of California at Berkeley in
1964. In 1966, Friedan founded the National Organization
for Women (NOW), which has continued the fight for equal
rights for women into the twenty-first century.

Excerpted from Betty Friedan, *It Changed My Life: Writings on the Women's Movement.*
Reprinted with permission from Curtis Brown, Ltd.

Women all over this country are on the verge of completing the massive delayed revolution that needs to be won for women. It is a delayed revolution because all the rights that would make women free and equal citizens of this country, persons able to develop to their full potential in society, were won on paper long ago. The last of these rights, the right to vote, was won the year before I was born [in 1920]. But we are not really free and equal . . . if the only world we really are free to move in is the so-called woman's world of home; if we are asked to make an unreal choice no man is ever asked to make; if we think, as girls, that we have to choose somehow between love, marriage and motherhood and the chance to devote ourselves seriously to some challenge, some interest that would enable us to grow to our full human potential.

Are we really free and equal if we are forced to make such a choice, or half-choice, because of lack of support from our society—because we have not received simple institutional help in combining marriage and motherhood with work in the professions, politics, or any of the other frontiers beyond the home? If girls today still have no image of themselves as individual human beings, if they think their only road to status, to identity, in society is to grab that man—according to all the images of marriage from the ads, the television commercials, the movies, the situation comedies, and all the experts who counsel them—and if therefore they think they must catch him at nineteen and begin to have babies and that split-level dream house so soon that they never have time to make other choices, to take other active moves in society, to risk themselves in trial-and-error efforts, are they, are we, really free and equal? Are we confined by that simple age-old destiny that depends only on our sexual biology and chance, or do we actually have the freedom of choice that is open to us as women today in America?

I say that the only thing that stands in women's way today is this false image, this feminine mystique, and the self-denigration of women that it perpetuates. This mystique makes us try to beat ourselves down in order to be feminine, makes us deny or feel freakish about our own abilities as people. It keeps us from moving freely on the road that is open to us. It keeps us from recognizing and solving the small, but real problems that remain.

A New Image of Women

Whether you know it or not, you have—in your own lives, in your own persons—moved beyond this false image [by attending this lecture]. You yourselves deny the feminine mystique; you deny the very images of women that come at you from all sides. There are no heroines today in America, not as far as the public image is concerned. There are sex objects and there are drudges. We see this on television every day.

You here, however, are the new image of women: as person, as heroine. You live actively in society. You are not solely dependent on your husbands and your children for your identity. You do not live your life vicariously through them. You do not wait passively for that wise man to make the decisions that will shape your society, but move in and help shape society yourself, and begin to make it a more human world. You bridge that old, obsolete division that splits life into man's world of thought and action and woman's world of love. With little help from society, you have begun to make a new pattern in which marriage, motherhood, home-making—the traditional roles of women—are merged with the possibility of women as individuals, as decision-makers, as creators of the future.

But because of the feminine mystique, you have not felt fully free and confident even as you have moved on this road. You have felt guilty; you have endured jeers, sneers, snickers, perhaps not from your own husband—who, I suspect, supports you more than the image would admit—but from the image-makers, and perhaps from your less adventurous neighbors, who are less willing to assume the role of heroine.

Your presence here today, however, is a testament to the fact that you are beginning to become conscious of the task that is before you. You are beginning to become conscious of the moment in history in which you stand, and this consciousness is what we need now. . . .

You know that you have brains as well as breasts, and you use them. You know what you are capable of, but you could use it for yourselves and for other women with so much more freedom if you could only break through those self-denigrating blocks. It is not laws, nor great obstacles, nor the heels of men that are grinding women down in America today. . . . We must simply break through this curtain in the minds of *women* in order to get on with the massive delayed revolution. And there *are* massive numbers of us. . . .

New Creative Work

I am speaking not only of the women who work outside the home in industry, but of every woman who works in society, for they all have made a certain advance from the isolation of household drudgery. Unfortunately, far too many women are taking jobs too soon in order to put their husbands through law, engineering, graduate or theological school, because these women do not take themselves and their own abilities seriously enough to put themselves through schools. Consequently, too many women of the one-out-of-three who work outside the home are concentrating on the housework jobs of industry—which are going to be replaced by the machine, anyway, just as much of the drudgery of our housework at home has been replaced by the machine. Even more of this household drudgery could be done by machines if the massive resources of American technology were devoted to it, instead of to selling women things they do not need and convincing them that running the washing machine is as creative, scientific and challenging as solving the genetic code.

All of these women in industry housework, however, are now in a position, with the proper training, to move ahead to the kinds of work that cannot be replaced by the machine. With them in the massive revolution are the great numbers of women who engage in volunteer community leadership, work that requires a great deal of human strength, thought and initiative. To a certain extent, their work is often more in tune with the rapid change in our society than that of the existing professions. Committed, innovative volunteer work is done almost completely by women in America, and thus is not recognized for what it is by our society. Therefore, by sneaking around the corner, it manages to innovate in ways that the conformity, the resistance to change, structured into the existing professions does not permit. . . .

Move into Politics

I would add also to the massiveness of this revolution the great numbers of women who are doing the housework of politics, who. . . acquiesce merely to lick envelopes, take nominal posts in ladies' aid auxiliaries, collect furniture for auctions, and second nominating speeches. Freed from their self-denigration, however, they could hold policy-making positions, run for the county committee, serve on the town committee, run for the state Senate or Congress, go to law school and become a judge, or even run for Vice President. I won't say President, for I think that may be premature, but it might help the revolution if a woman had enough courage to try. Above all, women in America need higher aspirations in politics. We know more than we think we know politically, and we are not using this knowledge.

Of all the passions open to man and woman, politics is the one that a woman can most easily embrace and move ahead in, creating a new pattern of politics, marriage and motherhood. Only self-denigration stops women in politics.

In addition, there are the great number of women who could be artists, who *are* artists but do not take themselves seriously as such. In *The New York Times* recently, there were some interesting figures that showed an enormous increase in the number of Americans who answered "Artist" on the census blank, who defined themselves professionally as painters, sculptors, art teachers, writers, poets, playwrights, television writers, all the rest. This great increase was almost completely made up of men. All that keeps a woman of talent from being an artist is her false image of herself, the fear of making the commitment to discipline herself—and of being tested. She doesn't even run across the problems that an American woman has, say, in wanting to become a physicist. Even if as a young girl she does not absorb the notion that physics is unfeminine, she may find it hard to want to have children and go to the physics laboratory at the same time. However, you can paint at home. It is only for lack of taking herself seriously that a woman who paints does not become an artist—or that a woman who wants to become a physicist doesn't work out some sort of accommodation for both children and a career.

Face the Future

I also add to the massive, delayed revolution many of the young women who. . . married early. They thought that all they had to do was to get that man at nineteen and that would take care of the rest of their life, and then they woke up at twenty-five or thirty-five or forty-five with the four children, the house and the husband, and realized they had to face a future ahead in which they would not be able to live through others. Such a woman, whose children are already moving out the door, finally asks herself what she is going to do with her life, and begins, even if late, to face and make some choices of her own. These great numbers of women are now trying to go back to college to get the education they gave up too easily and too soon, and they are getting more or less—too often less—a helping hand from the educators. Some of the universities are breaking through formal barriers and helping these women to grow to their full potential by admitting them to part-time college or graduate work—since part-time study is usually the only answer today for a woman who is still responsible for small children. Some universities may even provide part-time nursery schools so that women may continue to study even during those years; in this way they will not emerge as displaced people when their last child goes off to school, and they will not have to contribute to the population explosion by having baby after baby for lack of anything else creative to do. Perhaps the colleges and universities will even begin to be a little less rigid and understand that a woman who has had the strength to innovate in the community—who has led in solving new problems in education, politics, mental health, and in all the other problems that women have worked on in their suburbs and cities in recent years—may have learned something that is the equivalent of an academic thesis.

See Through the False Image

Finally, there are the great numbers of young girls for whom, thank heaven, the choices are still ahead. If they only see through the false image [society paints of women], they can so easily make the little choices—not the false big ones such as marriage versus career, but the little ones—that, if made all along, will easily create a new image of woman. And even if their choices involve effort, work, a few conflicts and problems that have to be solved, these are easier problems than that desperate emptiness a woman faces at thirty-five or forty after she realizes that all her life cannot be lived in lifelong full-time motherhood. These young girls can decide in high school "I would like to be a physicist, I would like to be a teacher, I would like to be a nurse, I would like to be an astronaut." Not "What do you want to be, little girl?" "I would like to be a mommy." "What do you want to be, little boy?" "I would like to be a cowboy." Of course he is going to be a husband and father; of course she is going to be a wife and mother. But the choices she must make in school are to learn what else she can be and do herself, because if she does not make these choices when she is young, she will not even try to do the work, to make the effort that will take her to our new frontiers.

The Antiwar Movement Is Born

James Miller

When Lyndon Johnson committed thousands of combat troops to fight in Vietnam in 1964, he created opposition of extraordinary proportions. Never before in American history had so many people vehemently opposed a war waged by the United States. For this reason, organized leftist groups fought among themselves as to the best tactics to use for protest. All were fearful of being labeled "Communist sympathizers" because such an affiliation carried very real consequences at the time—members of such groups faced the loss of jobs and careers and increasing hostility from the general public.

Nonetheless, the antiwar movement grew rapidly, led by "New Left" groups such as the Students for a Democratic Society (SDS), a campus organization that had previously protested against the plight of blacks in the South and now began to speak out against the growing conflict in Vietnam. SDS leaders such as Tom Hayden, Rennie Davis, Abbie Hoffman, and Jerry Rubin quickly became national leaders of the antiwar movement.

When the United States began bombing North Vietnam in 1965, the debate over tactics was secondary to the urgency of stopping the war. In those early days, protesters naively thought that by picketing the White House and sending an antiwar petition to Congress the fighting would cease and the United States would withdraw from Indochina.

In the following excerpt, James Miller writes about the birth of the antiwar movement and the debate between vari-

Excerpted from James Miller, *Democracy in the Streets: From Port Huron to the Siege of Chicago.* Reprinted with permission from Sagalyn Agency.

ous groups over tactics and strategy at the SDS's December 1964 National Council meeting in New York City.

Miller is the editor of *The Rolling Stone Illustrated History of Rock & Roll* and a book and music critic for *Newsweek.*

It must have been a relief to hear the plainspoken [political writer] I.F. Stone crisply marshal his facts and offer his arguments in his address to the National Council. Though his topic was "America and the Third World," Stone talked mainly about the war in Vietnam. He presented a brief history of the escalating military involvement in Southeast Asia, and eloquently argued that it was time for the United States to get out.

The National Council meeting resumed the following day to hear Paul Booth and Todd Gitlin present their proposals for the Peace Research and Education Project. After quickly approving a sit-in in March against the Chase Manhattan Bank to protest its investments in South Africa, the group opened debate on Vietnam.

Stone's speech had convinced a number of members of the need to protest the war—but there agreement ended. Gitlin proposed that SDS [Students for a Democratic Society] write and circulate a declaration "to this effect: 'I won't be drafted until the U.S. gets out of Vietnam.'" Jeff Shero suggested instead that SDS raise medical supplies and send them to the "Viet Cong by U.S. mails"—a bit of symbolic bravado that was typical of Shero's style. . . . The debate began to heat up. Was SDS pro-Communist? How could it endorse any action without first trying to educate its student constituency?

Clash Over Tactics

Discussion shifted to Gitlin and Booth's "Draft Resolution on Vietnam." Their resolution called on the President "to withdraw American troops from their undeclared war, and to use American influence to expedite a negotiated neutralist settlement in that beleaguered country." The group rejected the resolution, but then went on to discuss possible amendments. Gitlin reintroduced his "I won't be drafted" proposal, but it was defeated when Jim Brook . . . resorted to a bit of parliamentary subterfuge and introduced a substitute motion. He proposed that SDS sponsor "a march on Washington during spring vacation."

Some immediately rejected a march as too tame. Others argued that a march would be too difficult to pull off and that it would monopolize too much energy, jeopardizing the group's multi-issue approach and diverting resources. . . .

At last Tom Hayden spoke. Summoning his best Zen style, he derailed the discussion with a series of sweeping questions, raising doubts about the wisdom of mounting a major anti-war effort. The matter came to a vote, and the proposal for a march was narrowly defeated.

The proponents of a march were unwilling to admit defeat. During a brief break in the meeting . . . those in favor of protesting the Vietnam War lobbied hard for support. They succeeded in persuading Bob Ross, who had voted with Hayden, to change his mind, and to reintroduce the motion for a march.

This time the proposal passed—barely. The meeting quickly agreed that SDS would be the sole organizational sponsor, but that any group could join. . . . Unable to reach consensus on a specific demand—unilateral withdrawal, negotiation and United Nations supervision were all discussed—the group finally approved a laconic statement: "SDS advocates that the U.S. get out of Vietnam. It so advocates for the following reasons: a) The war hurts the Vietnamese people; b) The war hurts the American people; c) SDS is concerned about the Vietnamese people and the American people."

Responsibility for planning the march fell to Booth, Gitlin and the New York office of SDS. "All expectations are that it will be a big thing," wrote Booth a few weeks later. How big he could scarcely have guessed.

During the first week in January, letters went out inviting any interested groups to join the SDS march on April 17,

Easter weekend. By the middle of January, I.F. Stone and Senator Ernest Gruening had both agreed to speak at the march. The smaller Marxist-Leninist groups quickly indicated their support. But mainstream organizations . . . held back. In a series of meetings in January . . . prominent older peace activists expressed their misgivings. They were unhappy that SDS had assumed sole sponsorship of the march, upset at the involvement of Marxist-Leninist [Communist] groups and critical of the failure to present a clear alternative to the administration's Vietnam policy.

While negotiations with . . . mainstream peace groups dragged on, the significance of the march suddenly changed. On February 8, 1965, after an American air base in South Vietnam had been attacked by the "Viet Cong," as Americans called the guerrillas of the National Liberation Front in the South, U.S. planes began to bomb targets in North Vietnam. On February 11, the new U.S. policy of "sustained reprisal" was officially announced by President Johnson.

Across the country, small protests spontaneously erupted. In San Francisco, 300 students marched in front of the main branch of the post office, demanding a cease-fire and withdrawal of U.S. troops. In St. Louis, students staged a sit-in at the Federal Court House. At the University of Minnesota, the student government passed a resolution calling for U.S. withdrawal. In Washington, D.C., 7 people began a "fast for peace" in the George Washington University cafeteria, while on Capitol Hill, Senator Wayne Morse deplored a "black page in American history." In Cleveland, SDS President Paul Potter sent a telegram to President Johnson: "Sane men in capitals throughout the world today are hoping and praying that you will not escalate this mad war further." And in Berkeley, Paul Booth delivered an impromptu speech on the steps of Sproul Hall—he was on the West Coast scouting out the prospects for organizing defense workers and trying to bolster the profile of SDS in the area.

Though Booth was preoccupied with planning [an unrelated] SDS protest . . . talk of Vietnam began to dominate his correspondence. "The number of spontaneous Vietnam demonstrations [is] very large," he wrote on March 5. "All the other peace groups are calling off their Easter Marches to support our demonstration. We are really the only thing moving, but we are moving very very rapidly. . . ."

Agitation Grows Bolder

Meanwhile, anti-war sentiment on campuses around the country continued to intensify. On March 24, a group of teachers and students at the University of Michigan, including a large number of SDS . . . members, staged an all-night "teach-in" on the Vietnam War. The idea was widely imitated at schools around the country throughout the spring.

The style of SDS agitation grew bolder. A poster showing a Vietnamese child badly scarred by napalm was printed with the message "WHY ARE WE BURNING, TORTURING, KILLING THE PEOPLE OF VIETNAM? . . . TO PREVENT FREE ELECTIONS." The national office mailed out a song sheet, with new lyrics set to civil rights songs: "And before I'll be fenced in," went one, "I'll vote for Ho Chi Minh, Or go back to the North and be free."

Paul Booth moved to Washington to take on the task of coordinating the march. "My first job," he says, "was opening an office. What a mess that was. . . . We spent hours cleaning out debris. We installed phones, negotiated with the National Park Police [for a March Permit], coordinated all the logistics. I became one of the small number of people who know all the things you have to worry about when you organize a march on Washington."

Early in April, President Johnson committed more U.S. ground troops to Vietnam and ordered them to take the offensive. Although he tried to conceal these developments from the public, skepticism in Congress was mounting. Senators Frank Church and George McGovern came out against the war. Hoping to assuage his critics, the President directed his aides to draft a major speech.

On April 7, 1965, Lyndon Johnson spoke at Johns Hopkins University. His text took a carrot-and-stick approach. The United States "will not be defeated," he declared—but he was ready for "unconditional discussions" with North Vietnam. Reaching into his pork barrel, he even offered to cut the Communists in on a U.S.-financed development project on the Mekong River. (In private, Johnson was more candid. "I'm not going to pull up my pants and run out of Vietnam," he bellowed at one liberal critic the day before his speech: "Don't you know the church is on fire over there?")

The SDS response to Johnson's speech was swift, savage—and under the circumstances, remarkably shrewd. In a press release on April 8, the organization accused the President of "conning" the American people. It pointed out that Johnson had failed to offer a cease-fire, although the North Vietnamese had made this a precondition of any negotiations. It poked fun at his plans for building a "Mekong River [Project]." It ridiculed his assumption that "push-button conspirators at mythical command posts" in Hanoi, Peking and Moscow generated revolutionary insurgencies in the Third World—as if "real and deep grievances" had nothing to do with it. Johnson's speech, the SDS statement concluded, was simply an attempt to make the administration's "obstinacy look like conciliation, its unreason look like reason, its war look like peace."

Liberal Backlash

Many older peace leaders were not yet prepared to draw that conclusion. Unamused by SDS ditties about Ho Chi Minh and appalled by posters of burnt babies, they found both the tone and the content of the SDS press release offensive. After all the backbiting and confusion of the previous weeks, some of them wanted simply to pull out and denounce the march; an attempt had already been made to dissuade Senator Gruening from speaking. Others wanted to lend the event carefully qualified support. After long debate at a last minute meeting, several of the most prominent older peace activists . . . finally agreed to issue a statement that expressed general sympathy with the SDS march, deplored "particular positions expressed by some of the elements in the march" and applauded the President's speech of April 7 for raising "the possibility of a healthy shift of American policy" in Vietnam. Despite its blandly conciliatory tone, this statement became the pretext for a caustic editorial about the SDS march which appeared shortly afterward in *The New York Post*—at the time, a bastion of liberal opinion. "Several leaders of the peace movement," declared the *Post*, "have taken clear note of attempts to turn the event into a pro-Communist production." But "especially in the aftermath of Mr. Johnson's call for unconditional negotiations, there is no justification for transforming the march into a frenzied one-sided anti-American show."

The statement and accompanying editorial recalled the quarrel between SDS and the League for Industrial Democracy in the summer of 1962. Once again, two generations of the left were at odds. Once again, a series of misunderstandings had helped to poison relations. Once again, the issue was anti-Communism.

But this time, the conflict was out in the open, in full view of the mass media. This time, the old issue of "united frontism" was real: SDS *had* entered into a temporary alliance with Marxist-Leninist groups. And this time, a number of older radicals and liberals quickly leaped to the defense of SDS. As a result, SDS was in no danger of collapsing under an onslaught from its critics. On the contrary: popular support for the march continued to mushroom.

The First Major Anti-War March

The march took place on a sunny spring day. Two weeks before, SDS had expected perhaps 10,000 people to participate. More than 15,000 showed up—some estimates ran as high as 25,000. This was no small circle of friends: this was the germ of a mass movement.

The day began with a picket outside the White House. "By 11:30," wrote Paul Booth in his report on the march, "the picket line completely encircled the White House." At 12:30, the crowd started to march toward the grounds of the Washington Monument. "As the marchers filed in," wrote Booth, "Phil Ochs, Bill Frederick, and the Freedom Voices sang about the war and what we would do with the peace if it could be won."

The first speaker was SNCC [Student Nonviolent Coordinating Committee] field-worker Bob Parris (Moses), who had recently stopped using his (real) last name in one of the most striking gestures of self-abnegating democratic (anti-)leadership in the Sixties. (He did not want to be regarded as a political messiah like the biblical Moses.) Parris maintained that the killing of peasants in Vietnam by American soldiers was morally and politically on a par with the killing of civil rights workers in the South by segregationists. "Use Mississippi not as a moral lightning rod," he said, "but if you use it at all use it as a looking glass.". . .

Staughton Lynd, a young Yale historian who had directed the Freedom Schools in the 1964 Mississippi Summer Project, talked about the activities of dissident faculty members around the country. He declared that he had refused to pay a part of his income tax, in protest against the war.

Senator Ernest Gruening criticized the Communist regime in Peking, but urged "the immediate cessation of our bombing in North Vietnam."

After Judy Collins sang Bob Dylan's "The Times They Are A-Changin'," a welfare mother . . . spoke. According to Booth's paraphrase, she said that "poor people in America are direct victims of the war in Vietnam, which is foreclosing the chances for a serious attack on poverty by wasting the money in Asia and by turning America into an armed camp."

What Kind of System . . . ?

The formal program had been carefully planned to end with the speech of Paul Potter, who at the time was president of SDS. "What we must do," declared Potter, "is begin to build a democratic and humane society in which human life and initiative are precious"—it was the special burden of his speech to express the larger political vision animating SDS. "The incredible war in Vietnam," said Potter, "has provided the razor, the terrifying sharp cutting edge that has finally severed the last vestige of illusion that morality and democ-

racy are the guiding principles of American foreign policy.
. . . What in fact has the war done for freedom in America?
It has led to even more vigorous governmental efforts to
control information, manipulate the press and pressure and
persuade the public through distorted or downright dishon-
est documents."

Potter climaxed his speech with a barrage of rhetorical
questions. "What kind of system," he asked, "is it that justi-
fies the United States or any country seizing the destinies of
the Vietnamese people and using them callously for its own
purpose? What kind of system is it that disenfranchises
people in the South, leaves millions upon millions of people
throughout the country impoverished and excluded from the
mainstream and promise of American society, that creates
faceless and terrible bureaucracies and makes those the place
where people spend their lives and do their work, that con-
sistently puts material values before human values—and still
persists in calling itself free and still persists in finding itself
fit to police the world? What place is there for ordinary men
in that system, and how are they to control it, make it bend
itself to their wills rather than bending them to its?

"We must name that system," said Potter, pausing for effect. Someone in the crowd yelled, "Capitalism." Others
shouted him down. Potter finished his thought: "We must
name it, describe it, analyze it, understand it and change it."

The speech brought the crowd to its feet. As have few documents before or after, Potter's speech managed to capture
the moral passion and restless questioning that constituted
the heart and soul of the early New Left. "I talked about the
system," he later wrote, "not because I was afraid of the term
capitalism but because I wanted ambiguity, because I sensed
there was something new afoot in the world that we were
part of that made the rejection of the old terminology part of
the new hope for radical change in America.". . .

Petitioning Representatives

After Potter's speech, the crowd surged toward the Capitol,
bearing a "Petition to Congress." "The problems of America

cry out for attention," declared the petition, "and our entanglement in South Vietnam postpones the confrontation of these issues while prolonging the misery of the people of that war-torn land. You must act now to reverse this sorry state of affairs. We call on you to end, not extend the war in Vietnam."

The form of the protest was orthodox—a group of citizens submitting a petition to their elected representatives. But the mood of the moment transcended its carefully calibrated symbolism. At a camp in Port Huron three years before, sixty people, after four days experiencing the pleasures of face-to-face political debate, had ratified a document [called the Port Huron Statement] calling for participatory democracy. In a handful of experimental projects in a few inner-city ghettos during the last twelve months, small circles of friends had probed the limits of democracy in practice, trying to change themselves, and to change America. Now they were marching with thousands of others on Congress. Walking 80 abreast, they clogged the Washington Mall. The vision of participatory democracy crystallized in a new experience, a new sense of power, a new sentiment of solidarity.

"It was unbearably moving," wrote Staughton Lynd a few weeks later, "to watch the sea of banners and signs move out from the Sylvan Theater toward the Capitol as Joan Baez, Judy Collins and others sang 'We Shall Overcome.' Still more poignant was the perception—and I checked my reaction with many others who felt as I did—that as the crowd moved down the Mall toward the seat of government, its path delimited on each side by rows of chartered buses so that there was nowhere to go but forward, toward the waiting policemen, it seemed that the great mass of people would simply flow on through and over the marble buildings, that our forward movement was irresistibly strong, that even had some been shot or arrested nothing could have stopped that crowd from taking possession of its government."

The first march against the war ended without incident. But for some young radicals, a new era of . . . hope had begun.

Chapter 2

War Protesters

Chapter Preface

In the 1950s, North Vietnam was ruled by an enigmatic dictator named Ho Chi Minh. His government was supported by the Communist nations of China and the Soviet Union, and China exerted a heavy influence on North Vietnam's affairs of state. The leader of South Vietnam, Ngo Dinh Diem, had weak support from his people, but was supported by the United States. Although Diem had pledged to hold democratic elections, he continued to resist such measures.

Within South Vietnam, Communists organized resistance to Diem's policies, which favored a small minority of land owners over a poverty-stricken populace. By the time Diem was overthrown in 1963, the North Vietnamese Communists, called Vietcong, were firmly entrenched within dozens of South Vietnamese villages.

In 1964, President Lyndon Johnson used the small skirmish in Vietnam's Gulf of Tonkin as an excuse to declare war against North Vietnam. The United States originally sent troops to train and supply the South Vietnamese army, but eventually American forces took over the war effort.

As the U.S. commitment in Vietnam grew, millions of Americans began to oppose the war. Some were members of traditional pacifist religious groups; some were long-time social activists who had marched for free speech and equal rights for African Americans. Many were young men who were afraid that they themselves might be drafted and sent to Vietnam to fight. On the fringes of these groups were a minority of revolutionaries who favored the Communist cause and had dreams of overthrowing the U.S. government.

Together, these people formed dozens of anti-war organizations made up of students, Vietnam vets who had fought in the war, celebrities such as folk singer Joan Baez, comedian Dick Gregory, and agitators such as Jerry Rubin who would later found the radical Yippie party. Taken together, this movement, although dominated by young white males, was racially and gender diverse, and united in their belief that the war was wrong.

To those who ran the government, the demonstrators were viewed as giving aid and comfort to the enemy. As a result, the FBI, CIA, and military intelligence began to illegally follow and harass demonstrators, tap telephones, open mail, and attempt to disrupt anti-war groups.

By the second half of the 1960s, the nightly news on television was dominated by pictures from Vietnam of burning napalmed villages, wounded U.S. soldiers, and peasants suffering the effects of America's intense bombing campaign. (By the end of the war, the tonnage of bombs dropped on Vietnam exceeded three times the total amount of U.S. bombs dropped during World War II.) By 1968, over one thousand Americans were being killed in Vietnam every month and popular opposition to the war mounted as the body count climbed. As voices in the media began to report that the war seemed unwinnable, resistance to the war solidified, and even former supporters of government policy began to question the U.S. commitment in Vietnam.

By this time, America's college campuses had become centers of the anti-war movement where local rallies, "teach-ins," and marches on Washington were organized. As a result, Americans had seen dozens of anti-war demonstrations in every major city. Many of the protesters were willing to go to great lengths to stop the war such as putting their bodies in the way of police clubs and tear gas. By the late sixties, anti-war protests had become so violent—and some protesters so radicalized—that it began to appear as if war was about to erupt on the streets of America.

What effect the anti-war movement actually had in ending the war continued to be debated long after the war had ended. Those who participated believed that by constantly calling attention to the immorality of the war through protest, they kept the issue on the front pages of the newspapers, eventually ending the war. Others believe that the

Americans boosted enemy morale and hardened Communist resolve. Whatever the case, the Communist commitment in South Vietnam was unwavering and they were prepared to fight indefinitely.

There is little doubt, however, that the vehement divisiveness of the war bled into other parts of American society and profoundly changed the social fabric of the United States for years after the last shot was fired in Vietnam.

"Vietnam Day" Protest in Berkeley

Jerry Rubin

In 1964, President Lyndon Johnson used a small naval skirmish in Vietnam between the North Vietnamese and the U.S. Navy to justify a massive military campaign in that small country. Almost as soon as American troops were ordered to Indochina, civil rights and free speech activists joined together to protest the American involvement in Vietnam. One of the earliest protests was held on October 15, 1965, near the University of California at Berkeley when tens of thousands of protesters attempted to close down the Oakland Army Terminal where recruits were shipped out for Vietnam. The umbrella organization for this activity was the Vietnam Day Committee (VDC), which was led by Jerry Rubin who had also been active in the Free Speech Movement (FSM).

In this excerpt from his book, *Do It!*, Rubin explains how he helped organize the first large peace march—called "Vietnam Day"—in Berkeley. The rally was a nonstop thirty-six hour teach-in which an estimated 25,000 people came to hear songs, speeches, and debates about the Vietnam War. Later, when he was called before the House Un-American Activities Committee (HUAC) for this action, Rubin attended the hearing dressed as a Revolutionary War soldier.

Rubin was evicted from the hearings for his costume, but drew widespread attention in the media for his antics. Learning from this, Rubin began to devise outrageous and extreme stunts that, while doing little to stop the war, made him the most visible member of the antiwar movement. Rubin later went on to become one of the founding members of the Youth International Party, or Yippies—an organization that used shock and humor to draw attention to Vietnam war protests.

After the violence at the 1968 Democratic Convention in Chicago, Rubin and six others were indicted for conspiracy to overthrow the government. Rubin was not convicted but the publicity from the trial made his revolutionary book *Do It!* a bestseller. Rubin was killed when he was hit by a car crossing a street in Los Angeles in 1994.

T he Vietnam Day Committee [VDC] was born while organizing the biggest teach-in in the history of the world, Vietnam Day, a 36-hour happening attended by 50,000 different people. That experience taught us to believe in the *Apocalyptic Action*.

History could be changed in a day. An hour. A second. By the right action at the right time.

Our tactic was exaggeration. Everything was "the biggest," "the most massive."

Our goal was to create crises which would grab everybody's attention and force people to change their lives overnight. . . .

An Emotional Hothouse

We were putting out a weekly newspaper, organizing door-to-door discussions about Vietnam in the black ghetto in Oakland, sending out speakers everywhere, leafleting soldiers at airports telling them to desert, advising young kids how to beat the draft, and coordinating research, petition drives, massive and mini-demonstrations. No government official could come to the Bay Area without being haunted by a VDC reception team of psychic terrorists.

There were always hundreds of people packed into five rooms, committee meetings going on everywhere and crazy activists who craved trouble planning super-secret projects in back rooms. In one room crazies planned to rent planes and fly over the Rose Bowl dropping antiwar leaflets on the crowd. In another room crazier people planned a direct assault on the Oakland Army Terminal.

The VDC was an emotional hothouse, perpetually in orgasm. It was no place to meditate.

The VDC became a legend across the world.

If you were *not with* us, you were *against* us.

We knew the day was not far off when there'd be Nuremberg Trials in Amerika and we'd be the judges.

We were fucking obnoxious—and dug every moment of it.

The politicians picked up our threat. They declared a State of Emergency and ordered the National Guard on alert. That organized our demonstration for us! Everybody came to Berkeley for the action.

Steve Smale, co-chairman of the VDC, went on TV to reveal the plans. What [grief] Smale caused the university! One of the world's most famous mathematicians and the most renowned professor at the university, here was Smale plotting and working with nonstudent crazies!

Smale said that the VDC would attack the Terminal by air (dropping leaflets from planes), sea (thousands of oarsmen in rowboats) and land (10,000 people marching from the campus through Oakland to the Terminal).

The governor replied that police dogs, tear gas and 3,600 troops would be ready to repel the invaders.

The Largest Demonstration

Meanwhile, across the country antiwar groups mobilized for action—the first International Days of Protest against the war in Vietnam. Demonstrations on the same day in every city in the country! From New York to Berkeley, everyone got ready for simultaneous orgasm.

Were Minutemen going to stand on rooftops and shoot into the crowd of Berkeley peace marchers?

Suspense dominated Telegraph Avenue.

Watts [the black ghetto in L.A.] had burned only two months earlier.

SHOWDOWN!

The teach-in was a bore. Too many words and not enough people. Only 4,000 were there, and our hearts sank.

But suddenly by seven o'clock that night, the campus was mobbed. Thousands of young people were pouring in from every direction. The largest crowd for a demonstration in the history of Berkeley!

Over 20,000 people!

The threats of the cops had not intimidated us!

We were going to end the war!

The teach-in speeches were still going on while the masses poured into the streets and began marching. The Steering Committee was caught on stage with its pants down, and committee members raced down side streets in an attempt to get in front of the marchers and lead them.

Ahead was the Oakland city limits and Oakland cops standing shoulder-to-shoulder across the street, armed with tear gas, clubs and police dogs.

As the march ebbed within three blocks of the war zone, the back of the line had not yet left the Berkeley campus. A massive line of humanity for 1½ miles from the campus to Oakland!

We were the bravest people in the whole world, our arms linked, singing, joyous.

Rumors filtered back:

"They got gas! They're going to tear gas us!"

None of us had ever been tear gassed before.

Debate broke out within the steering committee: what to do? turn left into Oakland? sit down? charge the lines? turn right back to Berkeley?

Turning Back

Behind us people shouted: *"Turn left! Turn left!* Oakland! Oakland!"

"We can't turn back," I said. "This is the greatest night in Amerikan history!"

"If we don't turn back, people are going to die. It'll destroy the movement forever!" said one Steering Committee member.

"*If we turn back*, it will destroy the movement!" Smale shouted.

"I don't want responsibility for somebody's death. We'll all be arrested. You can't run a movement from jail," another member said.

The chanting behind us grew louder: *"Left! Left!"*

Petition to End the War

On March 8, 1965, the first American combat troops arrived in South Vietnam. By the end of that month, teach-ins, sit-ins, and protests had been initiated on college campuses across the United States. The first nationwide demonstration against the war—the SDS-sponsored March on Washington—took place on April 17. More than 20,000 people attended the march. In the belief that a simple petition signed by average citizens would stop the war, the following petition was delivered to Congress.

We, the participants in the March on Washington to End the War in Vietnam, petition Congress to act immediately to end the war. You currently have at your disposal many schemes, including reconvening the Geneva Conference, negotiation with the National Liberation Front and North Vietnam, immediate withdrawal, and UN-supervised elections. Although those among us might differ as to which of these is most desirable, we are unanimously of the opinion that the war must be brought to a halt.

This war is inflicting untold harm on the people of Vietnam. It is being fought in behalf of a succession of unpopular regimes, not for the ideals you proclaim. Our military are obviously being defeated; yet we persist in extending the war. The problems of America cry out for attention, and our entanglement in South Vietnam postpones the confrontation of these issues while prolonging the misery of the people of that war-torn land.

You must act now to reverse this sorry state of affairs. We call on you to end, not extend, the war in Vietnam.

Quoted in *Who Spoke Up? American Protest Against the War in Vietnam 1963–1975*. Garden City, NY: Doubleday & Company, 1984.

"That's the fucking militants up front. They don't care what happens to the people behind them."

"Let's leave it up to the crowd," a militant said. "The nine of us can't decide for 20,000 people. Let's stop the march, get the loudspeaker and let the people debate what to do."

"That's completely demagogic. How can you have democracy in the streets with 20,000 people when you're going to be tear gassed any minute? The people who shout the loudest will get their way," replied the spokesman for the conservatives.

The chanting grew more insistent: TURN LEFT! TURN LEFT! TURN LEFT!

"People may be killed. I don't want the responsibility."

"A movement that isn't willing to risk injuries, even deaths, isn't for shit. We can't turn back because we're afraid someone may be killed."

The vote was 5–4 to turn back to Berkeley.

The banner swung to the right.

I fell back into the crowd, tears welling in my eyes.

Shock and puzzlement swept through the crowd. "What happened? This isn't the way to Oakland! Why are we going back to Berkeley!"

The joy and ecstasy that had rippled from soul to soul as we marched toward Oakland disappeared.

It became a funeral march.

Sad and solemn.

Fuck "leaders." Fuck "steering committees."

A movement that isn't willing to risk injuries, even deaths, isn't for shit.

Fighting the Hell's Angels

The next day 8,000 people showed up for a second try, this time in the afternoon. As we approached the line of Oakland cops, someone whispered "The Hell's Angels are at the line."

[Poet] Allen Ginsberg, clanging cymbals and singing *Hare Krishna* on the truck that headed the march, was worried. "I hope there won't be trouble," he said. "They're probably there to fight the police."

"Amerika first! Amerika for Amerikans! Go back to Russia, you fucking Communists!"

A blackjacketed Angel grabbed the banner at the head of the march and ripped it in two.

Fighting broke out all over between Angels and monitors. Panic. Monitors pleaded with the crowd, "Don't run. Sit down."

Club-swinging Berkeley cops moved in. One cop swung from left field and split open the head of a 300-pound, 6-foot, 6-inch Angel. Blood spurted.

Another Angel jumped a cop and broke his leg.

But the Angels were outnumbered and finally captured. They were loaded one by one into paddy wagons, and the peace marchers cheered the Berkeley cop with the broken leg as he was carried off in a stretcher.

A Theatrical Production

We vowed to march again on the Army Terminal in three weeks. But the overwhelming question was, "What if the Angels attack again?"

One night the Marxist left packed the VDC meeting and passed a resolution advocating arming and defending ourselves with clubs and defense guards.

The next night pacifists packed the meeting and passed a resolution saying, "If attacked, we will bleed."

Ginsberg came to the meetings with his own ideas:

we should announce in advance that psychologically less vulnerable groups like Women for Peace, grandmothers, naked girls, mothers, families and babies will be at the front of the march. If the Angels attack, everyone on the march should begin mass calisthenics.

we should immediately, en masse, sing "Three Blind Mice" or "Mary Had a Little Lamb."

at the first sign of disturbance, we should play over the PA system [the Beatles song]: "I Wanna Hold Your Hand."

every marcher should bring flowers and give them to the Angels, the police, the politicians and the press.

"A demonstration is a theatrical production," Ginsberg

said. "The life style, energy and joy of the demonstration can be made into an exemplary spectacle of how to handle situations of anxiety and fear/threat."

Judge Grants Permission

Could we get [Bob] Dylan to come and sing at the march? Ginsberg pondered for a second and said, "Dylan might come if the march says nothing about the war. Like if everyone carries a placard with a picture of a different kind of fruit."

Nobody knew how to handle Ginsberg's pre-yippie, acid ideas.

Oakland again denied a march permit. But a federal judge worked out a compromise: we couldn't close down the Oakland Army Terminal, but we could march to an Oakland park for a rally.

The Hell's Angels called a press conference. They announced they were going to spend the day getting drunk.

So the march came and went.

Twenty thousand people walked into Oakland with picnic baskets to hear after-dinner speakers in a march protected, ironically enough, by the Oakland cops.

The Oakland Mayor praised VDC monitors for their "responsible work."

Then all the people went their separate ways home.

The energy drained from the antiwar movement.

The VDC house rattled like an old skeleton.

One day a bomb blew half the building away.

The spirit once ours was restored to Mother Earth.

During the next two years, we tripped, made love and got to know ourselves, to prepare for our next life-or-death struggles against the war-makers: Oakland Stop the Draft Week and the Pentagon.

Meanwhile the war went on.

Vietnam Veterans Against the War

Richard Stacewicz

On April 15, 1967, the first mobilization against the war—organized across the country on college campuses—brought between 200,000 and 400,000 people out to march in the rain in New York City. About 50,000 marched in San Francisco, and other cities had smaller protests. There were many groups with different agendas who opposed the war in Vietnam. Perhaps those with the most insight into the horrors of the war were the Vietnam Veterans Against the War (VVAW), a group made up of former soldiers who had seen action in Vietnam. These vets, some in uniform and some in civilian clothing, marched at the front of these huge antiwar demonstrations.

Many of the vets had mixed feelings about the marches. Since so many civilians were dying in Vietnam, some in the peace movement called the veterans "baby killers." Others only wanted the vets to march in order to legitimize the peace movement in the eyes of the critics. And although most Vietnam vets opposed the radical positions of Yippies such as Jerry Rubin, the horrors of battle that they had experienced motivated them to do their part to end the war.

The media tended to focus on the hippies in the crowd but, according to this narrative by Jan Barry—one of the founding members of VVAW—the protesters were actually from a diverse cross section of America and included former soldiers, blue-collar workers, African Americans, Hispanics, housewives, and other patriotic Americans.

Excerpted from Richard Stacewicz, *Winter Soldiers: An Oral History of the Vietnam Veterans Against the War.* Copyright ©1997 Twayne Publishers. Reprinted with permission from The Gale Group.

When I got out of the Army, in May of 1965, [I] flew back to upstate New York and immediately came to New Jersey. There was a girl here I had been writing to and therefore decided to come to this region looking for a job. . . .

She went to a peace demonstration either in 1965 or early 1966 in New York. I wasn't in any way interested in going to this peace demonstration. She came back. I asked what happened, and she said some news person came up and asked why she was there and she really didn't have anything much to say. I remember being mad at her. "Well, why didn't you know why you were there? Why couldn't you say why you were there? Why couldn't you say what's wrong with the war?"

At that point, my sympathies were to research what was going on. I researched everything, from reading Mao Tse-tung in the original to what's behind their side of it, and whatever else I could get my hands on. I was taking college classes on Saturday, and I took economics. I did research into our economic relationship with South Vietnam. Out of this I learned that we were, in essence, turning it into an economic colony, turning a rice-exporting region into a place [where] we sell them rice. There were lots of articles in *Fortune* magazine and other kinds of places about these great deals that were being done.

I talked to people. Reporters started telling me they'd go out and interview the ones just coming back from Vietnam, [in] late 1965, early 1966, from the first larger wave that went in there, and "These guys are more bitter than you are."

At one point, I ran into one of these guys, and he was extremely bitter. He was the only survivor in a unit that was wiped out. He said, "Why the hell should I prop up this rotten society?" He disappeared and no one ever heard from him again.

That was the thing that propelled me to organize something, realizing that there were all these angry guys out there, so turned off from their own society that it was frightening. Somebody had to articulate why that anger was there, what that bitterness was about. I didn't know how, but I had to learn how to do that.

Reading Between the Lines

I remember toward the end of 1966 1 had finally reached a point of frustration. I decided to move to Manhattan and start looking for more compatible people. I didn't think [of] a peace movement. There were lots of people who were asking questions. They were thinking about raising the questions. None of these questions were visible in the news media that we worked for.

Things like "Johnson Goes on Peace Parley" would be the headline. You'd read the story, and it had nothing to do with a peace parley; it was a war parley. Everything was out of a Washington perspective. Even if the reporter from the *New York Times* or whatever was reporting from Saigon, the story got twisted around to be a Washington perspective. You learned how to read between the lines. The editors were doubting their own reporters in Vietnam. That was very clear to me. It all added up to: The American public has no idea whatsoever of the reality. How do you convey that reality when everything seems to be closed up?

I walked into the New York Public Library main branch one day, asked for the personnel office, and said, "I'd like to work here." I took a pay cut and took the job, filing things and all the rest of the stuff.

I discovered there were all these students from all the various colleges in New York who worked there, and they were talking about something [that] was going to happen in the spring. They were so out of it. We're talking about young students who had no idea about anything. This didn't lead me to want to get involved with them until I saw an advertisement in the *New York Times Book Review* from the Veterans for Peace, saying, "If North Vietnam stops bombing us . . . we'll be ready to negotiate" or something like that. It turned the whole thing around. They weren't bombing us. They weren't threatening us. "Join us, April 15th," I think it said, "at Central Park for the start of this march"—which was the first time, place, and invitation that I felt, Ah-hah, that appeals to me. I liked the way they turned the issue around, a twist on reality.

"Veterans to the Front!"

I went with a friend [and] several people from New Jersey. There was this mob scene. There was a huge number of people at Central Park, from Columbus Circle all the way back as far as you could see. One of the stories of the peace movement that still hasn't really been told was the diversity. It wasn't just this hippie image that has determined the legend. This demonstration that I'm seeing for the first time was full of families in their Sunday best and younger people. This was pre-hippie. People in 1967 still had straight, narrow ties. Look at all the civil rights people and the peace movement people of the time: suits and ties, short hair. I went there wearing a suit and tie and a raincoat.

As we're standing there wondering what to do next, there's this big cry, "Vietnam veterans to the front!" There's this huge group of disciplined people marching, wearing Veterans for Peace hats. At the beginning of this group of veterans someone had provided a banner, hoping some Vietnam veterans would show up. It said, "Vietnam Veterans Against the War." There were some guys already carrying the banner and there were some guys behind them. I just joined that group.

There were some young guys in parts of uniform, or suits and ties, and some women and children. I don't think there were more than a dozen Vietnam veterans and some family members; but behind them—which to me at the time was far more impressive—was like a regimental size, I think 2,000 guys, marching in military formation wearing Veterans for Peace hats.

When we proceeded out of the park and down through Fifth Avenue and through the various other streets, people were ready to lynch, howling and screaming and throwing things. First they see a little group of dignitaries, which apparently included Martin Luther King, Jr., [antiwar activists] Dave Dellinger, A.J. Muste, and a couple of other people carrying an American flag. They're way out there by themselves taking all this abuse. Then, there's this little band of people carrying a sign, "Vietnam Veterans Against the War." You heard this sea change in the crowd. "What is this? Is that for real? [Angry tone.] It can't even be for real. This has got to be a joke." Then behind that, this group that clearly is veterans. "What!" I mean, this isn't what they expected. "Who are these people? If they're involved, I've got to rethink my opposition to all these people, hollering and screaming at them." You literally could feel and hear a change in these sidewalk crowds. Of course, behind that came a crowd that was so huge [that] they filled up all the streets in midtown Manhattan over to the UN and blocked all the traffic. The entire plaza in front of the UN was filled. All the side streets were filled, and people were still coming. . . .

Forming an Organization

Then everybody left. I started asking around, "What happened to that veterans' group?" I found out when Veterans for Peace had a meeting, went to that meeting, and I discovered that there was no Vietnam veterans' group. They initially said, "You should join us." I thought that we would make more of an impression upon people, we'd have a better ability to articulate to people what's going on in Vietnam, if we stand as a Vietnam veterans' organization. I simply started asking where any other Vietnam veterans were.

By June 1st . . . we actually had our first organization meeting. I had names of maybe two dozen people. We formed an organization utilizing the same name that was on the banner. Dave Braum designed the logo, which we talked about. "Let's take that patch that has the sword going through the Great Wall of China and put the rifle with the helmet on it, which symbolized a dead GI. We're filling the Great Wall of China with dead GIs!" There was symbolism!

We started off with a structure that had officers and bylaws and very few people. The only titles we had were for the paperwork: president, vice president, secretary, treasurer. I didn't utilize that in most of the organizing. I would just say I was a member of the national executive committee. I did this deliberately so that somebody couldn't decide they could pop me off. I had seen a few assassinations going on. I thought, I'm not going to be a target. Somebody thinks they could just kill me and that's the end of the organization. In addition, my own sense of organizing was that these guys don't want one person telling them what to do. What they need is a process in which empowerment takes place.

One of the things that I find astounding about this whole process is, I think, that this society provides these ready-made forms of democracy that are there if you want to use them. So without even thinking about it, we formed a democratic organization rather than an autocratic organization.

Our first office was a desk in the corner of the Fifth Avenue Peace Parade Committee. We had support from Veterans for Peace. Many of us went to their meetings. They utilized their fund-raising network to raise money and get us off the ground. It was a lot of money. By 1968, we took an office of our own on Fifth Avenue. . . .

"How Many Babies Did You Kill?"

In the peace movement, you ran into attitudes that ranged from not knowing what to do with us to people who wanted to manipulate us in various ways. One of the first times I walked into the Peace Parade Committee, some woman who looked very much like my mother said, "And how many babies did you kill?"

The socialist groups were always trying to manipulate us, [to] get you to join their organization. Certain things would happen, but we were so unsophisticated or inexperienced that you didn't even realize that a number had just been run on you. You just knew that something was funny.

You go to a coalition meeting; somebody from some really radical black group says, "Fuck the Vietcong—I don't care about those Vietnamese. They never did nothing for me." Jerry Rubin is doing crazy things that have absolutely nothing to do with Vietnam but addressing his ego. Over in the other corner is somebody else who is babbling that the whole problem is sexism. That isn't keeping those people from dying every day to say that. What are we here for? This is a peace movement coalition meeting, right?

The whole point was to focus on what this crazy coalition was going to do for its next spring or fall offensive. That's what we do in the peace movement, because it used the students. It took six months to organize these monsters. They thought, Well, if we could get 100,000 people in Washington, that will end the war. If we get 200,000 people . . . if we get 500,000 people . . . then the moratoriums would get 1 million people to surround the White House, it will end the war.

I was much more interested in: Where can I go and talk to two, or three, or four conservatives, and change their minds? In the middle of all this, you had a group of veterans, who psychologically and politically were bouncing all over the place. . . .

An Organization Opposed to Violence

One of the reasons I felt so strongly about forming VVAW was to provide a forum for people to come to and utilize a platform. Other people came for all kinds of other reasons. What I found most remarkable is: Even with all these various places that people were coming from, it still grew to be fairly basic VVAW philosophy that we're going to do this nonviolently, which is remarkable. You're talking about people who had all been trained to kill people. Many of them did, repeatedly.

We were going to level with the American people and tell them things, even if they didn't want to hear about them, like war crimes. We discovered early on, when going around speaking, that you couldn't even touch on the subject [war crimes]. People didn't want to hear that. "There's no way that American boys would ever do something like that!" Everybody—liberals, conservatives—just cut it right off. You felt stunned. This is what had been the reality over there. You're simply reporting the reality, and people say, "No, it couldn't have happened."

We constantly talked about how you turn things around, imagewise. We didn't use the word "jujitsu," but it was the same kind of principle: to turn around a lot of things so people would turn around and say, "Wait a minute. What? What did you just say?" Get them to think about it. . . .

Educating the Public

When we first started out, there was a small number of people in VVAW, so it made sense that we go on television and talk programs and talk anyplace we could find an audience. Our goals were to educate the public to the reality of what was going on in Vietnam so a better decision could be made. We were calling for—I think the tag line of the thing was—"Save our buddies now; withdraw them now." No one else should die in a war that the American public didn't vote for. This wasn't really clear to people. There had been no vote on this war.

In that first several months, well into the beginning of 1968, our whole goal was to utilize those people we could get motivated, to do their research and speak. The average GI doesn't know all these facts. You can't simply say, "I was out there, but I don't know anything about the Geneva Convention; I don't really know about Ho Chi Minh; I don't really know about how we got into Vietnam." We insisted . . . that you get educated. . . .

None of us had a degree in political science. We had the same general sense as most people. You change the public attitude in this country, things change. It wasn't any grander than that.

To give you a sense of strategy. . .When we first started, we wore suits and ties. [It was] a conscious decision that we're going to show people that we're serious. At that time in American society, if you were a serious person, you wore a suit and tie to do serious business.

We had a big debate about whether or not to wear our uniform, because it was against the law to wear a uniform after you were no longer on active duty. I think the first demonstration that we all decided that yes indeed, if you wanted to do it, you could do it, was in April of 1968 in New York. Some people showed up in dress uniforms. We're

not talking about the grungy jungle shit. Full-dress uniforms. There's a couple of pictures around with guys standing with VVAW banners and flags in full-dress uniforms.
You can imagine the effect this had upon cops and lots of
other people. Holy shit! These people are for real—a whole
bunch of medals.

Refusing to Serve

David Harris

During the 1960s, it was the legal duty of every 18-year-old American male to register with the Selective Service System, or draft board for service in the armed forces. Every man was then given a draft card which he was required to carry with him at all times. Those who attended college or graduate school were given deferments, or postponements of their military service. This meant that those who had to fight in Vietnam were disproportionately poor, undereducated, and from minority backgrounds.

Many war protesters burned their draft cards or mailed them back to the Selective Service Administration in protest. Those who refused to fight were put in federal prison for several years.

David Harris was one such protester. After serving as student body president of Stanford University in 1966, Harris became a national leader in the antiwar movement. When he returned his draft card to the government, he was convicted of violating the Selective Service Act. Harris, who was married to folksinger Joan Baez, was forced to leave his pregnant wife and serve two years in a federal penitentiary. Harris is a journalist and author of seven books.

I was nineteen when I demonstrated against the war for the first time. It was the fall of 1965, when the first rotation of American troops was still settling in around Saigon and Da Nang [in Vietnam]. I had been in Mississippi the previous fall for a quick tour with the civil rights movement, vol-

Excerpted from David Harris, *Our War.* Copyright ©1996 David Harris. Reprinted with permission from Times Books, a division of Random House, Inc.

unteering in the effort to win black people the right to vote
. . . but the politics I had brought to it were minimal and had
grown only a little over the intervening year. I knew . . .
about the obstruction of free elections [in Vietnam], about
[North Vietnamese leader] Ho Chi Minh . . . [and South
Vietnamese leader] Ngo Dinh Diem. I knew about [the
deadly effects of] napalm. . . . I was, by then, eager to cross
the line into open opposition [to the war].

A Decade of Demonstrations

I remember the occasion was a march against the war,
staged in Berkeley, under the theme "Get out of Vietnam."
The original plan had been to march from the University of
California to the Army Supply Depot on the Oakland wa-
terfront, but the city of Oakland had denied a parade permit,
so we marched to the border, where a line of Oakland police were waiting in riot gear, and held a rally on the Berkeley side, where we were watched by the combined Oakland
and Berkeley police, plus a delegation of Alameda County
Sheriff's deputies. Perhaps five thousand people attended,
not counting cops, and some two hundred of those had driven up from Stanford, about equal parts student and faculty. A march the previous week along the same route had
been attacked by several members of the Hell's Angels motorcycle gang. The bikers were out along the sidewalk again
as we marched down the middle of the street, but nobody attacked. At the rally I remember a long-winded speech about
how the United States had violated the Geneva Accords as-
suring the decolonization, independence, and unification of
Vietnam. I caught a ride home afterward with a friend driving a VW van.

A decade of demonstrations followed: in front of federal buildings and outside napalm plants, induction centers,
military bases, defense laboratories, troop depots, boot
camps, airport gates, university auditoriums, think-tank
campuses, assorted courthouses both state and federal, and
both the Pentagon and the White House. I am still proud of
most of them.

Returning the Draft Card

They were all the same in a way: we were just looking for a chance to open the discussion and conduct the argument. We were convinced that once anybody started taking a hard look at what was going on out in the tall grass, he or she would come to abhor it as much as we did. That certitude was a blessing, to be sure, but, like everything connected with this war, it became its own kind of burden as well. Few who came of age in those days got off easy. I remember.

Joan Baez Protests to the IRS

In 1964, Joan Baez was a well-known folk singer who had sold several million albums. She was also prominent in the civil rights and antiwar movements. When Lyndon Johnson decided to escalate the war in late 1964, Baez protested by writing the following letter in which she refused to pay the estimated 60 percent of her income taxes that went to military research and armaments. She sent the letter to the Internal Revenue Service (IRS) and the press at the same time. For the next ten years, the IRS collected their taxes from Baez by seizing pieces of her property and taking the revenue from her concerts, but she was never arrested.

Dear Friends:
   What I have to say is this:
   I do not believe in war.
   I do not believe in the weapons of war.
   Weapons and wars have murdered, burned, distorted, crippled, and caused endless varieties of pain to men, women, and children for too long. Our modern weapons can reduce a man to a piece of dust in a split second, can make a woman's hair to fall out or cause her baby to be born a monster. . . .
   I am not going to volunteer the 60% of my year's income tax that goes to armaments. There are two reasons for my action. One is enough. It is enough to say that no man has the right to take another man's life. Now we plan and build weapons that can take thousands of lives in a second, mil-

The first step across the line felt like an emergence, from dark into light, from forest into clearing, instantly easing the groping pressure of trying first to suppress our disbelief and then, finally unable to suppress any longer, to endure the rub of mustering gumption sufficient to risk ourselves. Everyone in the Movement had a succession of those moments of initial elevation as each new risk was assumed. The one I remember best came in August 1966, some three months after I'd been elected student body president. I was living in a

---

lions of lives in a day, billions in a week.

No one has the right to do that.

It is madness.

It is wrong.

My other reason is that modern war is impractical and stupid. We spend billions of dollars a year on weapons which scientists, politicians, military men, and even presidents all agree must never be used. That is impractical. The expression "National Security" has no meaning. It refers to our Defense System, which I call our Offense System, and which is a farce. It continues expanding, heaping up, one horrible kill machine upon another until, for some reason or another, a button will be pushed and our world, or a good portion of it will be blown to pieces. That is not security. That is stupidity.

People are starving to death in some places of the world. They look to this country with all its wealth and all its power. They look at our national budget. They are supposed to respect us. They do not respect us. They despise us. That is impractical and stupid.

Maybe the line should have been drawn when the bow and arrow were invented, maybe the gun, the cannon, maybe. Because now it is all wrong, all impractical, and all stupid.

So all I can do is draw my own line now. I am no longer supporting my portion of the arms race. . .

Sincerely yours,
Joan C. Baez

Joan Baez, *And a Voice to Sing With*. New York: New American Library, 1987.

ramshackle house in East Palo Alto, about half a mile from the mud flats along San Francisco Bay. I shared the house with six others, but none of them was home. After thinking awhile, I sat at my typewriter and wrote a letter to my draft board back in Fresno. I enclosed my draft cards and told to whom it may concern at Local Board No. 71 that I would never carry them again, nor obey any of their orders as long as the war lasted. I sealed the envelope, walked down the block to the mailbox, and put the envelope in. I remember that summer afternoon, the dirt of the road shoulder, the enormous black walnut trees nearby, and I remember feeling like I could have flapped my arms and flown back to my house if I had wanted. I felt like I was my own man for the first time in my life.

Challenging My Government

I had, of course, jumped more than a few hurdles by then. I had not been raised to call attention to my complaints, so parading on a street to announce them to anyone who would listen was an extreme form of learned behavior. But I learned. I also learned to ignore the taboo against challenging the government in time of war. We all knew somehow that this was far too serious to stand back like that. In the early days, when there were only a very few of us in just a few places, most of us were liberated territory to one another. And there was not much else available. Estrangement from the norm was an almost universal condition among us, part of the disintegration the war spread all along the home front. The norm was dropping jellied gasoline [napalm] on the tree line and firing canister rounds into thatched huts [in Vietnam]; life as we had been raised to live it had turned out to be a function of the chain of command. So we had to invent new selves as well: not an easy task for anyone at any time but especially difficult when swimming upstream against both our government and our culture.

None of us should have had to make such choices when we did. We were too young, and the choices were too hard.

But we made them any-
way. It was part of our vic-
timization that we should
come of age at the crux of
our nation's moral fulcrum,
where it would be left to us
to stand up to the war on
which our elders had de-
cided to spend us. Most
were not especially pre-
pared for this role, but we
had to play it, writing the
script as we went along.
We had to deal with the
war, somehow figuring out
if we were going to have a
part in it or a part in stopping it and just what that
part should be. The stakes
were genuine, and the con-
sequence seemed enor-
mous. It was not some-
thing easily escaped.
Some choices were en-
forced, whether you made
them or not. If we did not

*People often burned draft cards at
antiwar demonstrations to show
their disapproval of the war in
Vietnam.*

act to make ourselves our own, we were the government's
by default. And the wages of being your own were severe.

Visit from the FBI

A year and a half after I sent my draft cards back, the FBI
came by to talk. Since the door was open, they walked in
without knocking. By then we had a printing press in the
garage and had been organizing civil disobedience against the
Selective Service System for more than six months, living
from cereal boxes, most of the time on the road in my Ram-
bler. The FBI said they were looking for David Harris. I said
I was he, though they seemed to know that already. They said

they wanted to talk. I said fine. They said out in their car, and I said fine again. They had me sit in the shotgun seat, with an agent behind the wheel and another behind me. They said I should know that whatever I said could be used against me. I said I had figured as much. They said they'd heard that I had been advocating that people violate the Selective Service Act. I said I certainly had and went through the previous month, day by day, providing places and times. I started to do the same for the month before, but the FBI said that was enough. They said they would be in touch.

A Short Step to Outlaw

I, of course, can never forget that the war was the law, and being against the war was treated as being against both. Nor should the rest of us forget it. That's just the way things were: to be young, scruffy, against the war, and outspoken was automatically to be treated as a suspect. From there it was a short step to outlaw, a step a lot of us made in a lot of different ways. And all those steps ended up a metaphor for the drift of the whole: we were forced to give up the comfort of the entrenched and the safety of silence and wander the badlands, looking for a place from which to hold off the forces of the tunnel without light at its end: outlaws of the heart at least.

We also have our own admissions with which to reckon: we sometimes drifted into the self-righteous, were plagued by a compulsion to push the envelope, to reinvent ourselves over and over again. We were faddists and could easily take ourselves too seriously and forget that our own position on the war had come at the end of a long and tormented personal migration. Too often our talk was cheap and our listening hard to come by. We latched onto simple truths no one else wanted to recognize and rode them until their wheels fell off. We were too quick to license all disbelief and too slow to reach outside our own presumptions. We were often too loud.

All that said, I still remember: we were also right.

Violence at the Democratic Convention

Tom Hayden

On August 24, 1968, as the Democrats assembled in Chicago for their presidential convention, more than 50,000 protesters from across the country descended on the city for what was billed by organizers as a week-long "Festival of Life" to protest the war in Vietnam. The event leaders planned to stage nonviolent protests against the war, picket the convention, and hold peace rallies in Grant, Lincoln, and Hyde Parks. The protesters hoped that their presence in Chicago would force the Democrats to take a position against the war which had been escalated under the Democratic administration of Lyndon Johnson.

Permits for the rallies were repeatedly denied by Chicago mayor Richard J. Daley. By the time the convention began, eleven thousand Chicago police were on full alert, ready to face off with tens of thousands of protesters who descended on the city. In addition to the police, six thousand National Guard troops were joined by seventy-five hundred fully armed U.S. Army troops along with hundreds of FBI, CIA, and army and navy intelligence officers.

The Democrats themselves were divided over the handling of the war. The man favored for nomination, vice-president Hubert Humphrey supported Johnson's policies in Vietnam. But another popular candidate, Minnesota senator Eugene McCarthy, opposed the war. This split flared into pushing,

Excerpted from Tom Hayden, *Reunion: A Memoir*. Reprinted with permission from Sarah Lazin Books.

shoving, and yelling on the convention floor as tensions mounted between police and protesters on the streets of Chicago. When the Democrats finally nominated the pro-war Humphrey, a nationally televised riot followed in which protesters, reporters, and even convention delegates were gassed and brutally beaten by Chicago police. The violence was quickly labeled by the media as a "police riot," since many innocent bystanders were beaten without cause.

Tom Hayden was at the center of the action when the riot began. Hayden was one of the founders of the SDS (Students for a Democratic Society) and was one of the leaders of the demonstration.

S uddenly there began a commotion by a flagpole situated between the bandshell and the police line. A shirtless longhair was climbing the pole toward the flag. Nothing seemed to madden the police more than affronts to the American flag, although their hearts never seemed to melt when we sang "America the Beautiful" or "This Land Is Your Land." On this occasion, the teenager on the flagpole intended to turn the Stars and Stripes upside down, an international distress signal, though no one knew his intention at the time. People at the foot of the flagpole were yelling their approval or disapproval. Led by Rennie,[1] our marshals headed over to keep order. A column of police waded in with clubs to make a forcible arrest. A few people threw stones and chunks of dirt at a police car. Dave[2] urged calm over the microphone. The vast majority remained in their seats as Carl Oglesby, the SDS president, was introduced. Carl was an extraordinary orator, and was saying that while we tried to give birth to a new world there were "undertakers in the delivery room" when thick lines of police, clubs in position, began forming in front of the flagpole, facing off against our marshals, who had largely succeeded in calming people down. Rennie later remembered taking the megaphone and telling the police it was under control, we had a

1. Davis   2. Dellinger

permit, and they should pull back to avoid further provocation. "On that last word," Rennie said, "they charged."

"Screaming, Fleeing, Stumbling"

The police started forward in unison, then broke ranks, running and clubbing their way through the marshals and into the shocked people sitting on their benches. Human bodies flipped over backward. Others staggered into the benches and fell. Some police stopped to beat again and again on their helpless forms, then moved forward into the screaming, fleeing, stumbling crowd. Tear gas was wafting into the air, and I saw Mickey Flacks running off with her baby's face covered. The police were the Gestapo to her. She approached several of them, screaming, "Here, do you want the baby? Take him, take my baby!" Gaining her control, she began shuttling injured demonstrators to the university hospital on the south side, with the baby asleep in a backseat carrier.

Somebody yelled to me that Rennie was hit and lay bleeding, trampled, and unconscious. Oglesby kept speaking, describing the police state unfolding even as he tried to exercise his freedom of speech and assembly. I was not disguised, so I took my shirt off to change my appearance for the moment. Then I turned over and piled up several park benches to slow the charge of the rioting police. Next I circled around the melee toward the flagpole area to check on Rennie. He was being attended to by our medics and readied for an ambulance. His head was split open and blood was flowing over his face and down his shirt. The man standing over him with a microphone and tape recorder, I later learned, was from Naval Intelligence. Rennie was taken to the hospital by our own medics. Within a short while, the police arrived at the hospital to arrest Rennie, who was beginning to recover from a concussion and abrasions. The hospital staff hid him under a sheet, rolled him on a gurney through the police lines, and placed him in a cab. He was driven to South Kimbark, where he watched the rest of the night's events from the Flackses' couch, his aching head heavily bandaged.

Somehow the insanity subsided after half an hour. The police pulled back to their original position, but now they were reinforced by new units and helicopters from every direction. National Guardsmen were moved into place by the bandshell as well, also taking up visible positions on nearby bridges and the roof of the Chicago Museum. Bleeding, gassed, and disoriented, we were now surrounded on all sides. A full force of twelve thousand police, six thousand army troops with bazookas and flamethrowers, and five thousand National Guardsmen with Daley dozers[3] stretched from the bandshell back to the Hilton[4] and the Loop.

"See You in the Streets"

Surprisingly, the rally went on, with Allen Ginsberg,[5] Dick Gregory,[6] and several other speakers. But eventually it came to a final focus. Dave Dellinger announced that there were options for people: first, joining himself in a nonviolent parade attempting to go to the amphitheater; second, staying, in the bandshell area; and third, moving out of the park for "actions in the streets." He then introduced someone from the Peace and Freedom Party who made the out-of-place proposal that we go picket with the striking Chicago transit workers. Next came a bizarre Jerry Rubin, with a live pig, which he wanted to enter in nomination for the presidency. A little flustered by these suggestions, Dave reiterated that his proposed nonviolent march would begin in the far corner of the park, and then he introduced me.

I was reaching a climax of anger and, curiously, freedom. It didn't matter what happened now. "Rennie has been taken to the hospital, and we have to avenge him," I began, repeating it twice to get people's attention. I pointed out the police, guardsmen, and droning helicopters, and warned that we were now surrounded as twilight approached. I urged people not to get trapped in the park, to find their way out and back toward the Hilton: "This city and the military ma-

---

3. armored Bulldozers   4. The Hilton Hotel was the site of the convention.   5. a poet
6. a black activist

chine it aims at us won't allow us to protest in an organized fashion. So we must move out of this park in groups throughout the city and turn this overheated military machine against itself. Let us make sure that if our blood flows, it flows all over the city, and if we are gassed that they gas themselves. See you in the streets."

Seconds later, I disappeared from the park with Bob Ross, heading for my . . . apartment and a new disguise. A *New York Times* reporter drove with us. I heard on the car radio that the Vietnam peace plank was rejected by the convention by a 1,500–1,000 margin and that a protest rally had begun on the convention floor. In about an hour, I was back at the bandshell with a fake beard and helmet to cover my face. It was late in the day, perhaps five o'clock. Dave's march of over a thousand people was half sitting, half standing, blocked by a line of police who would not let them out of the park. Meanwhile, individuals and small groups of demonstrators were headed north along the lakeshore chain of parks looking for a bridge to cross onto Michigan Avenue and access routes to the central downtown area. Each of the crossings was occupied by troops employing mounted machine guns and the Daley dozers.

"The Whole World Is Watching!"

By some miracle, our trotting, winding crowd finally came to an open bridge at Jackson Boulevard, north of the Loop, and with a great cry of liberation ran over the short space and into Michigan Avenue, turning left to head the mile back toward the Hilton. There were over five thousand people cheering, running, shaking fists or making V-signs, flowing like a peasants' army toward the castle of the emperors. Seemingly from nowhere, the mule-drawn Poor People's Caravan, which Dr. King[7] had intended to lead before his death, materialized in our ranks with Ralph Abernathy[8] leading it as we headed down Michigan Avenue. It was seven-thirty, nearly time for Humphrey's nomination.

7. Dr. Martin Luther King Jr.   8. an African American leader

The streets were open, as the police were forced to regroup into the face of our surprising initiative. The Dellinger march disintegrated, and everyone found their way toward the Hilton.

It was nearly dark, the city lights turning on, as we reached the corner of Michigan and Balboa, where all the swirling forces were destined to meet. Lines of blueshirts were in front of us, clubs at the ready. The protest column filled the street and swelled with unity as we moved straight ahead now. The first lines sat down.

As if by magic, hands were suddenly in the evening air, and we began chanting, "The whole world is watching, the world is watching, the whole world is watching."

Gas, Clubs, and Kicks

We saw smoke and heard popping noises a split second before tear gas hit our front lines and began wafting upward into the Hilton and nearby hotels. We stopped, choking, trying to bite into our shirts. Then the blueshirts charged, chopping short strokes into the heads of people, trying to push us back. They knocked down and isolated several people, leaping on them for terrible revenge. One very young longhair was caught in the gutter, four or five police cutting his head open with their clubs. A reporter took a famous picture of him, face bleeding, holding up the V-sign, before he passed out. Medics wearing Red Cross armbands, who tried to get to him and others, were clubbed, choked, and kicked down in the street. Mace was squirted in the face of any others who approached, including the photographers. The mass of people fell back, stunned but orderly, helping the injured, to regroup for another march forward. . . .

I got through the front lines and around the police to the very wall of the Hilton, where a mixed group of fifty or so McCarthy workers, reporters, protestors, and—for all I knew—plain ordinary citizens, were standing frozen against the wall, between the hotel and the police, who were facing the oncoming marchers. When the marchers fell back, the police turned on our trapped crowd, moving in with a vengeance, clubs and Mace pointed at our faces. We instinctively joined arms. They started pulling off one person at a time, spraying Mace in their eyes, striking their kidneys or ribs with clubs, and tripping them. Their eyes were bulging with hate, and they were screaming with a sound that I had never heard from a human being. Someone started shouting that a woman was having a heart attack. We were so besieged that I couldn't turn around to see what was happening. Then, as people started staggering backward, someone kicked in the window behind us, and we fell through the shattered street-level opening to the Hilton's Haymarket Lounge (named, strangely enough, in memory of Chicago police killed by an anarchist's bomb during a violent confrontation between police and protestors in 1886). The police leaped through the windows, going right by me, turning over tables in the swank lounge, scattering the drinkers, breaking glasses and tables.

Beating Convention Delegates

Now, the *inside* of the Hilton was a battleground. Trapped demonstrators were trying to sit inconspicuously—in Levi's and ripped shirts—in chairs in the lobby until it was possible to get out safely. Bloody victims were walking about dazed, looking for help, as bellboys and clerks stared in shock. Reporters were rubbing their heads and trying to take notes. The McCarthy forces started bringing the injured to a makeshift "hospital" on the fifteenth floor, where they had headquarters. It had been a very bad night for them. The candidate's wife, Abigail, and children were warned by the Secret Service not to attend the convention; she assumed this was because they could not be protected from the Chicago police.

Upstairs now, the staff members of the defeated presidential candidate[9] were ripping up bed sheets to serve as bandages. Many of the wounded were their own. Some flipped-out political aides were throwing hotel ashtrays at

9. McCarthy

the police down in the street; others were trying to pull them away. Lights all over the McCarthy floors of the Hilton were blinking on and off in solidarity with the protestors in the streets below. Soon, the police cut the phone lines to the McCarthy suites and, in a final orgy of vengeance, stormed the fifteenth floor, dragging sleeping volunteers out of bed and beating them up as well. . . .

A Tunnel with No Light at the End

I had reached exhaustion; so had the protest. So too had the hopeful movement I had hoped to build only a few years before. Over the course of the next day, the defiance wound down. Dick Gregory led a march halfway to the amphitheater before it was stopped by more arrests, this time of many convention delegates themselves. We heard Eugene McCarthy, with gentle dignity, urge us to "work within the system" to take control of the Democratic party by 1972. He was harangued embarrassingly by SDS leader Mike Klonsky as a "pig opportunist." Ralph Abernathy spoke from an impromptu stage, an upside-down garbage can, calling it a symbol of Martin Luther King's last cause.

I lay on the grass, pondering the alternatives. Reform seemed bankrupt, revolution far away. We had taught the pro-war Democrats the lesson that business as usual was a formula for political defeat and moral self-destruction. But was anybody listening?

I felt drawn into a tunnel of our own, with no light at its end.

The National Commission on the Causes and Prevention of Violence, appointed by President Johnson, concluded that a "police riot" was to blame for the disaster. In his introduction to the report, *Los Angeles Times* reporter Robert J. Donovan described the Chicago police behavior as nothing less than a "prescription for fascism."

Drawing on twenty thousand pages of witness statements, most of them from the FBI and the U.S. Attorney's offices, and 180 hours of film, Walker's team came to conclusions at great variance from Daley's accounts. There were 668 arrests during Convention Week, most of them involving individuals under twenty-six years of age, the vast majority being young men from Chicago with no previous arrest records.

About 425 persons were treated at the movement's makeshift medical facilities. Another two hundred were treated on the spot by movement medics, and over four hundred received first aid for tear gas. A total of 101 required treatment in Chicago hospitals, forty-five of those on the climactic night of the twenty-eighth.

There were twenty-four police windshields broken, and seventeen police cars dented (by whomever). In addition, 192 of eleven thousand officers checked themselves into hospitals. Of this number, 80 percent were injured in the spontaneous events at Michigan and Balboa on the twenty-eighth. Only ten police, according to their own affidavits, said they were kicked, six said they were struck, and four said they were assaulted by crowds.

In contrast, of three hundred press people assigned to cover the street actions, sixty-three (over 20 percent) were injured or arrested. Fifty (including Dan Rather) were struck, sprayed with Mace, or arrested "apparently without reason," in the words of the Walker Report. The Daley machine had tried to sharply limit television access to the convention and streets; when that failed, the whole world was watching their tactics.

Chapter 3

Hippies and the Psychedelic Revolution

Chapter Preface

While protesters fomented revolution in the streets, the Haight-Ashbury neighborhood in San Francisco was the birthplace of a more peaceful—and longer-lasting—social revolution. When LSD research spilled out of top-secret government laboratories and onto city streets around 1965, it unleashed a wave of psychedelic madness that transformed America almost overnight. Led by rock bands such as Jefferson Airplane and the Grateful Dead, and acid gurus such as Timothy Leary and Ken Kesey, the socially conservative atmosphere of the early sixties was suddenly fractured by an unprecedented drug-induced revolution against traditional American values.

As tens of thousands of mostly white middle-class teenagers followed Leary's advice, "turned on, tuned in, and dropped out" and became hippies, they began to ridicule their parents' world for what they saw as its materialism, blind patriotism, and devotion to hard work.

Men grew long hair and beards, women donned peasant dresses, "granny glasses," and love beads. Any and all traditional social practices were challenged, including marriage, child rearing, and religion. Buddhism, Hinduism, and other Eastern religious practices including meditation replaced mainstream religion for some. The birth-control pill allowed women the freedom to experiment sexually for the first time in an era before AIDS. Hundreds of people moved onto communes where they pooled their money and shared their resources. Fueled by the widespread availability of marijuana and LSD, millions of people bought a ticket into this new world of free love and free thinking.

There was, however, a dark side to the revolution. Hippie neighborhoods in big cities filled with thousands of very young people who had no jobs and expected to survive by panhandling quarters on street corners. Many of these innocent young teenagers were preyed upon by criminals who gave them addictive drugs like heroin. Some women were forced into prostitution.

By the late sixties, a great exodus began in the hippie neighborhoods. Hippie innovations such as organic health food, environmentalism, and relaxed social mores were quickly accepted by mainstream American culture as the people of the counterculture took what they had learned at "acid tests" and the Human Be-In and applied it to their own lives.

The Birth of the Hippie Culture

Barney Hoskyns

San Francisco was the center of the hippie universe. The scene there began in 1964 when hundreds of small groups of friends found a common bond in the taking of LSD, or "acid." At the center of the acid movement was the author of *One Flew Over the Cuckoo's Nest*, Ken Kesey, whose group of Merry Pranksters toured the country high on LSD in a wildly painted bus.

By 1965, novice rock promoters were bringing thousands of like-minded individuals together at giant psychedelic "Acid Tests" where hundreds of people would take LSD (which was still legal) and dance the night away to the music of Jefferson Airplane, Grateful Dead, and other groups. The counterculture scene that began in San Francisco soon spread across America and even around the globe, leaving the legacy of the sixties with a colorful and unique identity.

In the following excerpt, music writer Barney Hoskyns describes the beginnings of the hippie movement in San Francisco. Hoskyns is an Oxford University graduate who has written several books about music and film, including *Waiting for the Sun: Strange Days, Weird Scenes, and the Sound of Los Angeles*. He has also written for *Rolling Stone, Times* (London), *Request*, and *Musician*.

In the summer of 1963, royalties from the acclaimed [*One Flew Over the*] *Cuckoo's Nest* . . . paid for a big log house in the hills of La Honda, northwest of Palo Alto. Here Ken Kesey and his compadres really went for it: Isolated within six acres in a mountain creek, they were free to pursue their [LSD] chemical experiments out of eyesight and earshot, wiring up equipment and speakers in the house and in the redwoods surrounding it so they could groove to [jazz great] Rahsaan Roland Kirk records while chopping wood. Kesey gradually began to abandon writing, seeing it as an essentially reductive and [middle-class] exercise and instead embracing something altogether more primordial and existential.

Everything now came down to the crucial experience of LSD, which made it impossible to continue to live by the straight world's games. When Kesey's tough, larger-than-life pal Ken Babbs returned from active duty as a helicopter pilot in Vietnam, the Merry Pranksters were born, and things became rapidly more intense and maniacal. The Pranksters bought a 1939 International Harvester school bus which had already done service for a family man who'd adapted it for the use of his eleven offspring (with bunks and benches and a sink and so forth), and daubed it with psychedelic swirls and patterns and endowed it with intense spiritual significance. The bus was to become a center and a symbol for the Pranksters: You were either on it or off it, cosmically speaking. The Pranksters embarked in the summer of 1964 on an insane, sleepless, paranoid odyssey that took them all the way through the deserts of the Southwest to Texas and New Orleans and then up to New York City for the publication of Kesey's second opus, *Sometimes a Great Notion,* all the while filming their escapades and encounters with straight America. At the rear of the bus hung a sign: CAUTION: WEIRD LOAD; at the front, its destination board read: FURTHUR—with two "u"s. . . .

Acid Changed Everything

Acid changed everything in San Francisco, and the Pranksters were evangelical to the point of zealotry in their attempts to turn people onto it. "Nobody was on any spiritual quest back then," recalled Ellen Harmon, a partner of

Chet Helmes' in the concert-promotion collective known as the Family Dog. "What it was, was getting away from mother and father so you could do whatever you wanted—which, in most cases, was just lying around and getting as high as you could! Then what happened was, everybody took a bunch of acid and got all *wired*. That's what happened to the scene! They got serious!" Acid was a dividing line between the old and the new, between the old Beat scene and the new youth counterculture. Beat veterans used the pejorative term "hippies"—ironically a term black musicians coined for white beatnik hangers-on in the jazz scene—to describe middle-class kids slumming it in North Beach, but it only betrayed how threatened they felt now that they were no longer running the show. Change was in the air, and the folkies who were in their early twenties knew they had to establish their own scene.

With North Beach becoming expensively gentrified, a number of coffeehouses and hip clothing stores began to open in Haight-Ashbury, a blue-collar, ethnically mixed neighborhood east of Golden Gate Park that was also home to students from the creative hotbed of San Francisco State University. The Blue Unicorn coffeehouse opened in early 1964, and by the summer "hippies" were shedding traditional beatnik garb and wearing the crazier clothes they found in funky [stores]. . . .

The new styles of flowing locks and robes went hand in hand with the new acid consciousness. . . . The Haight's new psychedelic disciples were seeing the world anew, casting off clothes and attitudes that had acted like straitjackets through their repressed adolescences. Life in the Haight took on a zany, freaky, anarchic quality.

A New Kind of Music

Contemporaneous with these mini-revolutions in everyday life was the new sound of electric rock'n'roll, breaking free of sanctimonious folk protest songs on the one hand and sappy, vapid teenypop on the other. Spearheading rock's revolution were the Beatles, whose hits initially met with scorn on the Bay Area folk circuit but were now making the hippie contingent rethink their stance. With the new wave of British invasion bands taking America by storm, and even Bob Dylan flirting with the ghost of electricity, folkies defected en masse. "The Beatles came along and that was pretty much it," noted Darby Slick of the Great Society. "Folk music just went instantly into the dumper." Slowly, as 1964 turned into 1965, acid began to penetrate pop. By December '65, [the Beatles'] *Rubber Soul* was the Haight's soundtrack. . . .

"One day the idea was there," recalled [Grateful Dead guitarist] Jerry Garcia. "'Why don't we have a big party and you guys bring your instruments and play, and us Pranksters'll set up all our tape recorders and bullshit, and we'll all get stoned?' And that was the first Acid Test . . . right away we dropped completely out of the straight music scene and just played the Tests." Here is the turning point for San Franciscan rock: A band that could theoretically have gone the Top 40/AM Radio/*American Bandstand* route but instead turned away and boldly decided to throw in their lot with a bunch of acid-guzzling renegades in La Honda—renegades, moreover, who by now had been busted for pot and were busily courting the most notorious of all California's subcultural tribes, the Hell's Angels. At a big La Honda party for the Angels on August 7, 1965, the fearsome bikers of Oakland consorted with such guests as Allen Ginsberg—who, as a Jewish New York intellectual homosexual, must have been close to everything an Angel would abominate—and the new acid superdealer Augustus Owsley Stanley III, source of the purest and the best LSD in the world.

Owsley rejoiced in many nicknames—the Bear, the Naughty Chemist, the White Rabbit—and manufactured millions of tabs of LSD. Some say that he kept his prices low, and even gave away as much as he sold. But he could afford to be generous: When LSD was still legal, he was able to buy a 500-gram consignment of the basic constituent of LSD, lysergic acid monohydrate, for $20,000, and turn it into a million-and-a-half doses wholesaling at about $1.50 a piece. In Tom Wolfe's words he was a "cocky little guy, short, with dark hair, dressed like an acid head, the usual boho gear, but with a strange wound-up nasal voice. . . ." At the height of his fame he was thirty years old.

Ordered Chaos

The first "Acid Test," if you could even call it that, took place in a somewhat desultory and disorganized manner at Ken Babbs' house in Santa Cruz, in the fall of 1965. "It started off as a party," wrote Tom Wolfe, "with movies flashed on the walls, and lights, and tapes, and the Pranksters providing the music themselves, not to mention the LSD.". . .

"When it was moving right, you could dig that there was something . . . like ordered chaos," remembered Jerry Garcia. "Everybody would be high and flashing and going through insane changes during which everything would be demolished . . . so there would be this odd interchange going on, electroneural connections of weird sorts." The [Grateful Dead's] decision to become a sort of house band for the Acid Tests . . . was one of the key events in the evolution of the San Francisco scene. Equally important was their decision to attend the second dance staged by Chet Helms' Family Dog collective on October 24. "What this scene needs is us," muttered an acid-flashing [Grateful Dead bass player] Phil Lesh as he wandered amidst the psychedelic throng at the Longshoremen's Hall. . . .

Acid-Spiked Kool-Aid

[The Family Dog dance at the Longshoremen's Hall] is where it all came together: Where the heads crawled out from the woodwork and discovered each other, where the new hippies realized to their amazement that they actually did constitute a community of sorts and did view the world together through the new lenses of acid consciousness. This is where the soaring folk-rock of the Airplane was heard for the first time outside the [nightclub] Matrix, and where the band's future singer Grace Slick made her first real mark with the Great Society. This is where Ralph Gleason—a forty-eight-year-old, cheroot-smoking, jazz journalist—met a pushy young Berkeley student named Jann Wenner, planting the seed that would become *Rolling Stone* magazine; and where John Cipollina met Gary Duncan and Greg Elmore and talked about founding the Quicksilver Messenger Service.

The Family Dog threw two further dances that fall: "A Tribute to Sparkle Plenty," headlined by the Lovin' Spoonful, and "A Tribute to Ming the Merciless," headlined by L.A.'s Mothers of Invention. Memorably described on its poster as "a Wham-bang, wide open stoned DANCE flicking on at dusk," "A Tribute to Ming the Merciless" sadly degenerated into a series of ugly brawls—bad vibes all round. Altogether more harmonious was the benefit show for the San Francisco Mime Troupe staged on November 6 by a hyperenergetic Berlin-born Jewish refugee [and future rock promoter] named Bill Graham. . . .

Graham never forgot the sight of the queue stretching along Howard Street on November 6, 1965, waiting to get into the Mime Troupe loft to see the Jefferson Airplane, the Mystery Trend, the Fugs and others play the appeal. He'd had no idea there were so many of these underground groovers out there, primed for multimedia frolics and rock-'n'roll that wasn't just teenage party music. Inside the loft there were films being projected on the walls, and fruit dangled from the ceilings. Booze and acid-spiked Kool-Aid were dispensed from garbage cans lined with aluminum foil. . . .

The Trips Festival

THE ACID TESTS WERE GETTING SERIOUS. The second one, held in San José on December 4, 1965, was flooded with kids who'd spilled out of the Rolling Stones' show that night at the San José Civic Auditorium. Tom Wolfe called it "the first mass acid experience," and *Whole Earth Catalog* founder Steward Brand noted that THERE WAS A DISTINCT "WHIFF OF DANGER" IN THE AIR. No less a personage than Owsley Stanley III showed up for the third Test at Muir Beach Lodge in Marin County on December 18. Ironically, "the Bear" had a bad trip—a hallucinogenic horror-show for which he ever after blamed Ken Kesey.

On January 8, 1966, the Acid Test finally came to San Francisco—to the Fillmore, to be precise. It was the city's first taste of the Pranksters' psychedelic bombardment—what [media critic] Marshall McLuhan termed "sensory overload" and Haight historian Charles Perry called "an overpowering simultaneity." Paramount in the spectacle was a new kind of dancing, relaxed, trippy, flowing with the hypnotic groove of the music and the colors and shapes brought on by the acid. "The Tests were thousands of people, all hopelessly stoned, all finding themselves in a room full of other thousands of people, none of whom they were afraid of," said Jerry Garcia, whose band played the Fillmore that night. Rave culture starts here. In the Fillmore audience was Rock Scully of the Family Dog, who'd been unwise enough to schedule a dance that very same night at the California Hall across town. . . .

The Fillmore Test, broken up by cops at 2:00 A.M. despite the fact that LSD was still perfectly legal, turned out to be merely a prelude to an altogether more ambitious happening dreamed up by *Whole Earth* [*Catalog*] visionary Steward Brand and artist Ramon Sender, and staged at the Longshoremen's Hall on the weekend of January 20/21, 1966. The Trips Festival, as it was dubbed, was the culmination of the Tests and the Mime Troupe appeals—the ultimate Test, the Test gone truly public. Billed as "a new medium of communication and entertainment, a drugless PSYCHEDELIC EXPERIENCE," it brought together the many strands of the Bay Area revolution: Musicians, dancers, S.F. State students, Berkeley activists, Open Theatre actors, Ron Boise and his Electric Thunder sculptures, and above all the Merry Pranksters, to whom Brand and colleagues offered the Saturday night as an Acid Test. "The general tone of things has moved from the self-conscious Happening to a more JUBILANT occasion where the audience PARTICIPATES because it's more fun to do so than not," the organizers wrote in their announcement. "Maybe this is the ROCK REVOLUTION." It was.

Come the Saturday night, the Pranksters were in their element: Ken Babbs ensconced amidst a huge agglomeration of pipes and platforms in the center of the hall, supervising the many projectors and flashlight machines, Neal Cassady lurching around in a gorilla costume, the fugitive Kesey encased inside an enormous space helmet. Paul Krassner of the *Realist* described what he saw as "a ballroom surrealistically seething with a couple of thousand bodies stoned out of their everlovin' bruces in crazy costumes and obscene makeup." Also wandering around in the midst of the madness was a man who struck Bob Weir of the Dead—and almost everyone else—as "an asshole with a clipboard." It was Bill Graham, who'd been hired to maintain some semblance of order but who was feeling thoroughly freaked out by his first experience of the Pranksters at work.

"Bill didn't have a clue," remembered Owsley. "I realized he was half-terrified by what it was and was doing everything he could to control it and suppress his realization that there was something special going on here." To Graham's disbelief and everyone else's, the Trips Festival made a profit of $16,000: It turned out this hippie shit could actually *pay.* More to the point, it kicked off the brief golden age of San Francisco, before the tourists and the record companies swooped down on the place. In the words of Tom Wolfe, "the Haight-Ashbury era began that weekend."

Spreading the Psychedelic Message

Timothy Leary

By the mid-1960s, LSD was the counterculture's drug of choice and even college professors and intellectuals were experimenting with it. No one was more visible in the national media than Timothy Leary, a former Harvard University clinical psychology professor, whose message "Turn on, tune in, and drop out," was taken to heart by millions of Americans. Hundreds of rich and famous Americans made the pilgrimage to Leary's rambling estate in Millbrook, New York, where they dressed in flowing Indian robes, practiced Eastern meditation, and wore flowers in their hair while Dr. Leary introduced them to the mental rollercoaster rides provided by LSD.

Leary believed that LSD could save the world by raising the consciousness of the human race. To spread his message he gave this interview to *Playboy* magazine in September 1966. The government, however, was less than happy with Leary's message. At the time of this interview, the psychedelic guru was facing thirty years in prison for possession of a minute amount of marijuana.

PLAYBOY: How many times have you used LSD, Dr. Leary?

LEARY: Up to this moment, I've had 311 psychedelic sessions.

PLAYBOY: What do you think it's done for you—and to you?

LEARY: That's difficult to answer easily. Let me say this:

Excerpted from Timothy Leary, *Politics of Ecstasy.* Copyright ©1980, 1985, 1993, 1998, Timothy Leary, Ph.D. Reprinted with permission from Ronin Publishing, Berkeley, CA, www.roninpub.com.

I was thirty-nine when I had my first psychedelic experience. At that time, I was a middle-aged man involved in the middle-aged process of dying. My joy in life, my sensual openness, my creativity were all sliding downhill. Since that time, six years ago, my life has been renewed in almost every dimension. Most of my colleagues at the University of California and at Harvard, of course, feel that I've become an eccentric and a kook. I would estimate that fewer than 15 percent of my professional colleagues understand and support what I'm doing. The ones who do, as you might expect, tend to be among the younger psychologists. If you know a person's age, you know what he's going to think and feel about LSD. Psychedelic drugs are the medium of the young. As you move up the age scale into the thirties, forties and fifties, fewer and fewer people are open to the possibilities that these chemicals offer.

PLAYBOY: Why is that?

LEARY: To the person over thirty-five or forty, the word "drug" means one of two things: doctor-disease or dope fiend-crime. Nothing you can say to a person who has this neurological fix on the word "drug" is going to change his mind. He's frozen like a Pavlovian dog to this conditioned reflex. To people under twenty-five, on the other hand, the word "drug" refers to a wide range of mind benders running from alcohol, energizers and stupefiers to marijuana and the other psychedelic drugs. To middle-aged America, it may be synonymous with instant insanity, but to most Americans under twenty-five, the psychedelic drug means ecstasy, sensual unfolding, religious experience, revelation, illumination, contact with nature. There's hardly a teen-ager or young person in the United States today who doesn't know at least one person who has had a good experience with marijuana or LSD. The horizons of the current younger generation, in terms of expanded consciousness, are light-years beyond those of their parents. The breakthrough has occurred; there's no going back. The psychedelic battle is won.

PLAYBOY: What do you say to the standard charge that

LSD is too powerful and dangerous to entrust to the young?

LEARY: Well, none of us yet knows exactly how LSD can be used for the growth and benefit of the human being. It is a powerful releaser of energy as yet not fully understood. But if I'm confronted with the possibility that a fifteen-year-old or a fifty-year-old is going to use a new form of energy that he doesn't understand, I'll back the fifteen-year-old every time. Why? Because a fifteen-year-old is going to use a new form of energy to have fun, to intensify sensation, to make love, for curiosity, for personal growth. Many fifty-year-olds have lost their curiosity, have lost their ability to make love, have dulled their openness to new sensations, and would use any form of new energy for power, control and warfare. So it doesn't concern me at all that young people are taking time out from the educational and occupational assembly lines to experiment with consciousness, to dabble with new forms of experience and artistic expression. The present generation under the age of twenty-five is the wisest and holiest generation that the human race has ever seen. And by God, instead of lamenting, derogating and imprisoning them, we should support them, listen to them and turn on with them. . . .

PLAYBOY: Is it necessary to have a guide [when taking LSD]?

LEARY: Yes. Unless you have an experienced guide—at least for your first 10 or 15 sessions—it would be confusing.

PLAYBOY: What if a person can't find either a guide or a source of LSD among his friends? Where does he go?

LEARY: LSD is against the law, and I certainly would not advise anyone to violate the law. I will say this, however: Throughout human history, men who have wanted to expand their consciousness, to find deeper meaning inside themselves, have been able to do it if they were willing to commit the time and energy to do so. In other times and countries, men would walk barefooted 2,000 miles to find spiritual teachers who would turn them on to Buddha, Mohammed or Ramakrishna. . . .

Ecstasy or Confusion?

PLAYBOY: What's it like [when you take LSD]? . . . What happens to you?

LEARY: If we're speaking in a general way, what happens to everyone is the experience of incredible acceleration and intensification of all senses and of all mental processes—which can be very confusing if you're not prepared for it. Around a thousand million signals fire off in your brain every second; during any second in an LSD session, you find yourself tuned in on thousands of these messages that ordinarily you don't register consciously. And you may be getting an incredible number of simultaneous messages from different parts of your body. Since you're not used to this, it can lead to incredible ecstasy or it can lead to confusion. Some people are freaked by this Niagara of sensory input. Instead of having just one or two or three things happening in tidy sequence, you're suddenly flooded by hundreds of lights and colors and sensations and images, and you can get quite lost.

You sense a strange powerful force beginning to unloose and radiate through your body. In normal perception, we are aware of static symbols. But as the LSD effect takes hold, everything begins to *move*, and this relentless, impersonal, slowly swelling movement will continue through the several hours of the session. It's as though for all of your normal waking life you have been caught in a still photograph, in an awkward, stereotyped posture; suddenly the show comes alive, balloons out to several dimensions and becomes irradiated with color and energy.

The first thing you notice is an incredible enhancement of sensory awareness. Take the sense of sight. LSD vision is to normal vision as normal vision is to the picture on a badly tuned television set. Under LSD, it's as though you have microscopes up to your eyes, in which you see jewel-like, radiant details of anything your eye falls upon. You are really seeing for the first time—not static, symbolic perception of learned things, but patterns of light bouncing off the objects around you and hurtling at the speed of light into the mosaic of rods and cones in the retina of your eye. Everything seems alive. Everything *is* alive, beaming diamond-bright light waves into your retina.

See the Music

PLAYBOY: Is the sense of hearing similarly intensified?

LEARY: Tremendously. Ordinarily we hear just isolated sounds: the rings of a telephone, the sound of somebody's words. But when you turn on with LSD, the organ of Corti in your inner ear becomes a trembling membrane seething with tattoos of sound waves. The vibrations seem to penetrate deep inside you, swell and burst there. You hear one note of a Bach sonata, and it hangs there, glittering, pulsating, for an endless length of time, while you slowly orbit around it. Then, hundreds of years later, comes the second note of the sonata, and again, for hundreds of years, you slowly drift around the two notes, observing the harmony and the discords, and reflecting on the history of music.

But when your nervous system is turned on with LSD, and all the wires are flashing, the senses begin to overlap and merge. You not only hear but *see* the music emerging from the speaker system—like dancing particles, like squirming curls of toothpaste. You actually *see* the sound in multicolored patterns while you're hearing it, At the same time, you *are* the sound, you are the note, you are the string of the violin or the piano. And every one of your organs is pulsating and having orgasms in rhythm with it. . . .

Ecstatic Energies

PLAYBOY: How about the sense of smell?

LEARY: This is one of the most overwhelming aspects of an LSD experience. It seems as though for the first time you are breathing life, and you remember with amusement and distaste that plastic, odorless, artificial gas that you used to consider air. During the LSD experience, you discover that you're actually inhaling an atmosphere composed of millions of microscopic strands of olfactory ticker tape, exploding in your nostrils with ecstatic meaning. When you sit across the room from a woman during an LSD session, you're aware of thousands of penetrating chemical messages floating from her through the air into your sensory center: a symphony of a thousand odors that all of us exude at every moment—the shampoo she uses, her cologne, her sweat, the exhaust and discharge from her digestive system, her sexual perfume, the fragrance of her clothing–grenades of eroticism exploding in the olfactory cell.

PLAYBOY: Does the sense of touch become equally erotic?

LEARY: Touch becomes electric as well as erotic. I remember a moment during one session in which Rosemary leaned over and lightly touched the palm of my hand with her finger. Immediately a hundred thousand end cells in my hand exploded in soft orgasm. Ecstatic energies pulsated up my arms and rocketed into my brain, where another hundred thousand cells softly exploded in pure, delicate pleasure. The distance between my wife's finger and the palm of my hand was about 50 miles of space, filled with cotton candy, infiltrated with thousands of silver wires hurtling energy back and forth. Wave after wave of exquisite energy pulsed from her finger. Wave upon wave of ethereal tissue rapture—delicate, shuddering—coursed back and forth from her finger to my palm.

PLAYBOY: And this rapture was erotic?

LEARY: Transcendentally. An enormous amount of energy from every fiber of your body is released under LSD—most especially including sexual energy. There is no question that LSD is the most powerful aphrodisiac ever discovered by man. . . .

Less Concern for Material Values

PLAYBOY: A great deal of what is said about LSD by its proponents, including you, has been couched in terms of religious mysticism. You spoke earlier, in fact, of discovering "divinity" through LSD. In what way is the LSD experience religious?

LEARY: It depends on what you mean by religion. For almost everyone, the LSD experience is a confrontation with new forms of wisdom and energy that dwarf and humiliate man's mind. This experience of awe and revelation is often described as religious. I consider my work basically religious, because it has as its goal the systematic expansion of consciousness and the discovery of energies within, which men call "divine." From the psychedelic point of view, almost all religions are attempts—sometimes limited temporally or nationally—to discover the inner potential. Well, LSD is Western yoga. The aim of all Eastern religion, like the aim of LSD, is basically to get high: that is, to expand your consciousness and find ecstasy and revelation within. . . .

PLAYBOY: According to a spokesman for the student left, many former campus activists who've gone the LSD route are "more concerned with what's happening in their heads than what's happening in the world." Any comment?

LEARY: There's a certain truth in that. The insight of LSD leads you to concern yourself more with internal or spiritual values; you realize that it doesn't make any difference what you do on the outside unless you change the inside. If all the Negroes and left-wing college students in the world had Cadillacs and full control of society, they would still be involved in an anthill social system unless they opened themselves up first.

Turn On, Tune In, Drop Out

PLAYBOY: Aren't these young ex-activists among an increasing number of students, writers, artists and musicians whom one critic has called "the psychedelic drop-outs"— LSD users who find themselves divested of motivation, unable to readjust to reality or to resume their roles in society?

LEARY: There *is* an LSD drop-out problem, but it's nothing to worry about. It's something to cheer. The lesson I have learned from over 300 LSD sessions, and which I have been passing on to others, can be stated in 6 syllables: Turn on, tune in, drop out. "Turn on" means to contact the ancient energies and wisdoms that are built into your nervous system. They provide unspeakable pleasure and revelation.

"Tune in" means to harness and communicate these new perspectives in a harmonious dance with the external world. "Drop out" means to detach yourself from the tribal game. Current models of social adjustment—mechanized, computerized, socialized, intellectualized, televised. . . make no sense to the new LSD generation, who see clearly that American society is becoming an air-conditioned anthill. In every generation of human history, thoughtful men have turned on and dropped out of the tribal game and thus stimulated the larger society to lurch ahead. Every historical advance has resulted from the stern pressure of visionary men who have declared their independence from the game. . . .

Communicating in New Forms

The reflex reaction of society to the creative drop-out is panic and irritation. If anyone questions the social order, he threatens the whole shaky edifice. The automatic, angry reaction to the creative drop-out is that he will become a parasite on the hardworking, conforming citizen. This is not true. The LSD experience does not lead to passivity and withdrawal; it spurs a driving hunger to communicate in new forms, in better ways, to express a more harmonious message, to live a better life. The LSD cult has already wrought revolutionary changes in American culture. If you were to conduct a poll of the creative young musicians in this country, you'd find that at least 80 percent are using psychedelic drugs in a systematic way, And this new psychedelic style has produced not only a new rhythm in modern music but a new decor for our discotheques, a new form of film making, a new kinetic visual art, a new literature, and has begun to revise our philosophic and psychological thinking.

Remember, it's the college kids who are turning on—the smartest and most promising of the youngsters. What an exciting prospect: a generation of creative youngsters refusing to march in step, refusing to go to offices, refusing to sign up on the installment plan, refusing to climb aboard the treadmill.

PLAYBOY: What *will* they do?

LEARY: Don't worry. Each one will work out his individual solution. Some will return to the establishment and inject their new ideas. Some will live underground as self-employed artists, artisans and writers. Some are already forming small communities out of the country. Many are starting schools for children and adults who wish to learn the use of their sense organs. Psychedelic businesses are springing up: bookstores, art galleries. Psychedelic industries may involve more manpower in the future than the automobile industry has produced in the last 20 years. In our technological society of the future, the problem will be not to get people to work but to develop graceful, fulfilling ways of living a more serene, beautiful and creative life. Psychedelics will help to point the way.

The Diggers Feed the People

Emmett Grogan

By 1967 articles about hippie culture had been published in magazines and newspapers across the country along with hundreds of photos of long-haired teens with flowers in their hair. As a result of this media blitz thousands of young people from across the nation made their way to Haight-Ashbury, San Francisco's hippie neighborhood. Unfortunately, these teenagers had no money, nowhere to live, and were easy marks for street hustlers and other criminals.

In response to this problem, a group of hippies formed an organization called the Diggers, named after a seventeenth-century English political faction who believed in free access to private lands for poor farmers. The San Francisco Diggers began feeding people for free every day in Golden Gate Park with food stolen or donated from commercial producers.

Emmett Grogan, along with his best friend Billy Landout, were the founding fathers of the Diggers. Grogan wrote (in the third person) about feeding the hippies in his autobiography *Ringolevio: A Life Played for Keeps.*

Billy and Emmett wanted to pull some sort of score which would benefit others besides themselves—some job that would provide a take big enough to share. Plain money wasn't the answer because greed would probably never permit a sizable cash haul to be properly divided among the people and besides, no one would learn anything about collective interaction from it. What was needed that they could buy with a sackful of stolen money?

"Bread!" exclaimed Emmett. He got Billy to drive his '55 Ford station wagon to the San Francisco Produce Market on the outskirts of the city. The sun had only been up for half an hour when they pulled through the chain-link front gate and drove into the lot, past the loading platforms stacked high with crates of fresh fruit and vegetables. One of Emmett's uncles used to truck wholesale produce from the West Side marketplace in Greenwich Village to some small supermarkets around Brooklyn, and at age ten or eleven Emmett had helped him quite a few times when his uncle's regular helper was sick. He learned his way around produce during those brief assists and stole meat from the same markets to pay for his junk [heroin] habit. Now he attracted a lot of attention because of his very long hair, but Emmett's fluent Italian compensated for that. He spoke with the immigrants who ran the wholesale stalls lining both sides of the market. At first most of them were suspicious, but they became friendly after he handed them a line, and within an hour the Ford wagon was packed tight with crates of food. There were tomatoes, turnips, green beans, cauliflower, brussels sprouts, onions, eggplant, squash, potatoes, lettuce, yams, apples and oranges. From a particularly generous Italian named Paddy, who managed the only poultry plant in the market, they got fifty pounds of chicken and turkey parts. That was all there was to it.

Free Because It's Yours

Driving back to town, they discussed different ways of distributing the food. The problem was that the street people, who really needed it, had no place or means to cook it.

"We can get it cooked. We'll make a stew."

"What do we use to cook with? What'll be big enough?"

"Cans."

"Cans? Garbage cans?"

"No, milk cans. They're sterilized 'n durable 'n you can handle 'em easy. "

So they snatched a pair of twenty-gallon milk cans from a dairy plant in the Mission district and transported everything back to Emmett's place. It was around 8 A.M., when they began boiling down the fowl to make a stock for the stew. They worked hard for hours preparing the vegetables, Emmett working as hard that first morning as he was going to daily for over a year. He worked harder than most blue-collar folks work for a living. . . . They talked while they worked and decided to give away the stew in the Fell Street Panhandle of Golden Gate Park at 4 P.M. that afternoon. While Emmett ladled the inches of grease away from the surface of the stock and continued to ready the greens, Billy went downtown to mimeograph and hand out several hundred leaflets notifying the Haight community about

> FREE FOOD   GOOD HOT STEW
> RIPE TOMATOES   FRESH FRUIT
> BRING A BOWL AND SPOON TO
> THE PANHANDLE AT ASHBURY STREET
> 4 PM   4 PM   4 PM   4 PM   4 PM
> FREE FOOD *EVERYDAY* FREE FOOD
> IT'S FREE BECAUSE IT'S YOURS!
> the diggers.

They added the greens and potatoes to the stock only minutes prior to leaving, otherwise they would have lost their solidity in the boiling hot soup and melted into a mush, instead of becoming a stew. It was just before 4 P.M. when the two of them drove over to the Panhandle and set the hot milk cans on the grass with the boxes of tomatoes and cartons of fruit. There were already fifty people waiting and another fifty-odd showed up immediately, some of them carrying their bowls tied to their belts. The number of people increased to a stationary two hundred, as the Free Food continued through the week in the Panhandle, every afternoon at four. The bowls dangling from the waistbands took on an immediately recognizable significance.

The word quickly spread and soon such underground papers as the Berkeley *Barb* were nibbling around, trying to scoop a story on who was behind the Free Food event. They only ended up running into an anonymous wall, and finally were discouraged enough to simply chalk it all up to that "mystery-shrouded Haight-Ashbury group, the Diggers." The hipsters who knew Emmett and Billy searched them out in the cold fog and found them sitting on the grass among the young newcomers to the Haight and the old-timers from skid row, gobbling up the soup du jour. The Hun [a director for the S.F. Mime Troupe] remarked that it was a great idea. "Try to keep it going for another week, if you can, and you'll really get your point across. Just another week. Terrific!" The straight New Lefties came around and turned a little green with envy that they hadn't thought of the food angle as an organizing principle themselves. If they had, they would have done it only as a one-shot for the publicity. The liberals, hip and square, would watch the hungry crowd being fed and grope around, looking for someone to offer a donation to. Conservatives would ask why everyone didn't get a job.

Burning $20 Bills

Emmett and Billy knew that Free Food everyday in the park was a popular act, but they didn't intend it solely as a symbol. No, they were hungry and so were a lot of others, and they were going to keep the Free Food going every day, in spite of everything and for nothing. When donors would offer notes of vicarious approval, they'd take the bills, strike a match, and burn them to the amusement of those eating. The young kids squatting in the Panhandle were hungry and afraid all right, but they were on their own for the first time for no matter how long, and they wanted no material support from members of their parents' world. The burning of the ten- and twenty-dollar bills typified, more than anything else, what they felt and what the Diggers believed.

A half-dozen young women, a few of whom were dropouts from Antioch College, shared a large pad together on Clayton Street and volunteered to take over the cooking indefinitely. Two other members of the Mime Troupe, Butcher Brooks and Slim Minnaux, undertook the everyday delivery of the prepared food to the 4 P.M. Panhandle feed. This left Emmett to make the early morning round of pickups at the Produce Market, the Farmers Market and the Ukranian Bakery. On his way back to Clayton Street every A.M., he would try to steal some beef for the stew. They didn't have access to any freezer storage space, so he could snatch only a side of beef at most from a meat packing plant, or from one of the trucks making deliveries, and take it back for the group to butcher themselves. He tried hustling a head butcher at the Allen Meat Company for a daily box of scraps and bones for soup stock, but he only got himself whacked on the head

The Death of the Hippie Concept

By 1967, San Francisco was flooded with media people attempting to write stories about hippies. People in the counterculture took advantage of the media spotlight to shock average Americans. In the autumn of 1967, after the so-called "Summer of Love," the Diggers staged a parade called "Death of Hippie," complete with mourners and coffins, which was covered by all the national media. The purpose of the event was to state that the media-created "hippie" was dead, and in its place was the "Free Man," whose image could not be controlled by newspapers, magazines, and television. The following explanation was distributed in Haight-Ashbury during the event.

OCTOBER SIXTH NINETEEN HUNDRED AND SIXTY SEVEN

MEDIA CREATED THE HIPPIE WITH YOUR HUNGRY CONSENT. BE SOMEBODY. CAREERS ARE TO BE HAD FOR THE ENTERPRISING HIPPIE. The media cast nets, create bags for the identity-hungry to climb in. Your face on TV, your style immortalized without soul in the captions of the [San Francisco] Chronicle. NBC says you exist, ergo I am. Narcissism, plebeian vanity. The victim immortalized. Black power, its transcendent threat of white massacre the creation of media-whore obsequious bowers to the public mind which they recreate because they too have nothing to create and the re-with the flat side of a cleaver—and no meat. Of course, he could have hijacked a whole trailer full of meat and fenced the goods, but that would have only been a one-shot deal, and the importance of Free Food was its steady continuance everyday at the same time for as long as it was needed.

The Free Store

Billy hustled some dough and Emmett rented a six-car garage on Page Street that was filled with empty window frames. He was joined by some young dudes from the 4 P.M. feed, who helped him nail the window frames all over the

---

flections run in perpetual anal circuits and the FREE MAN vomits his images and laughs in the clouds because he is the great evader, the animal who haunts the jungles of image and sees no shadow, only the hunter's gun and knows sahib is too slow and he flexes his strong loins of FREE and is gone again from the nets. They fall on empty air and waft helplessly to the grass.

DEATH OF HIPPY END/FINISHED HIPPYEE GONE GOODBYE HEH-PPEEEE DEATH DEATH HHIPPEE. . . .

YOU ARE FREE. WE ARE FREE. DO NOT BE RECREATED. BELIEVE ONLY YOUR OWN INCARNATE SPIRIT. Create, Be. . . . Do not be created. This is your land, your city. No one can portion it out to you. The H/Ashbury was portioned to us by Media-Police and the tourists came to the Zoo to see the captive animals and we growled fiercely behind the bars we accepted and now we are no longer hippies and never were and the City is ours to create from, to be in. It is our tool, part of the first creation which the FREE MAN creates his new world from.

BIRTH OF FREE MAN FREE SAN FRANCISCO INDEPENDENCE FREE AMERICANS BIRTH. . . .

DO NOT BE BOUGHT WITH A PICTURE, A PHRASE. . . . DO NOT BE CAPTURED IN WORDS. THE CITY IS OURS. YOU ARE ARE ARE. TAKE WHAT IS YOURS. . . . TAKE WHAT IS YOURS. . . .

Quoted in *New Notes from the Underground*. New York: Viking Press, 1968.

wooden front of the garage and clean up the inside. . . . They stenciled a sign below the roofline and opened the doors to the street within a few days. The place was called the Free Frame of Reference and it was the first free store.

Emmett didn't bother to make clear to the community something which was very important. He didn't bother because he didn't want to at the time. That something was that the Free Food was not begun to prolong the economic usefulness of day-old bread or vegetables or bad cuts of meat, and the free stores were not set up to prolong the economic usefulness of secondhand clothes and other items. Only a fraction of the goods used or accepted were secondhand and they were made available and displayed to effect a Salvation-Goodwill-salvage cover to conceal the fact that the rest of the stuff was new and fresh and had been stolen. People who tried to deposit their refuse at the Free Frame of Reference were told to go and recycle their garbage someplace else. And when the stiffs wanted to speak with whoever was in charge of the operation they were told, "You're in charge! You wanna see someone in charge? You be in charge!" This was done not only to dramatize the concept of assuming freedom, but also to prevent the cops from vamping and busting someone for being in possession or receipt of stolen property. For the same reason, the leases for these places were always signed by some drifter passing through town and not by Emmett or Billy or anyone else. No one ever accepted responsibility for anything.

Butcher Brooks was a photographer and he had a battered VW bus painted a bright yellow, with a slogan written on the outside panel in orange Day-Glo, "The Road of Excess Leads to the Palace of Wisdom!" He had been working as a Digger for about a month, and his bus became known around the streets as the yellow submarine, often carrying the Digger women—Natural Suzanne, Fyllis, Cindy Small, Bobsie, NanaNina—in the back with the prepared food. The crowd would see the yellow submarine coming down Ashbury Street and they would mill around near the curb in the park. Brooks sometimes felt the people were taking the Free

Food too much for granted so, instead of parking and un-loading, he often teased them by continually passing, until he sparked them into some sort of action, like waylaying the bus when it became delayed in traffic, removing the ignition keys, and seizing the cooked food. He also made them work for it by sealing the milk cans tight, banging the lids firmly shut with a hammer. It would take some time for several guys in the park to tug the jammed cover free of the blister-hot can and ladle out the stew. This Free Food theater evolved to a point where Billy constructed a giant, thirteen-foot square Frame of Reference from four two-by-fours bolted together, and Emmett painted it a golden orange. The frame would be set up between two large oak trees in the Panhandle every day before 4 P.M. When the Free Food arrived, it would be placed on one side of the frame and the hungry would be made to walk through it to get at the stew and whatever else was being shared on the other side, changing their frame of reference as they did.

From City Protesters to Country Communes

Marty Jezer

By the late 1960s, thousands of teenagers from across the
nation were pouring into big-city hippie neighborhoods. This
influx of humanity gave rise to homelessness, poverty, and
the use of hard drugs such as heroin. These factors combined
to destroy the feelings of peace and love that the hippie
movement was founded on. In response to these negative factors, thousands of people abandoned the cities in order to "get
back to the land," on communal farms.

Marty Jezer was a Vietnam War protester who started a
counterculture magazine called *Win* in New York City. The
violence associated with the anti-war movement alienated
many protesters, including Jezer. At the same time, he found
a sense of community and sharing with others who held the
same political beliefs. As Jezer saw the peace movement
begin to engage in head-on battles with the government and
police, he decided to buy a farm with a few friends and start a
commune in Vermont.

P rivate property . . . lost its value. We took to opening our
houses to the many [peace] movement people who always seemed to be passing through New York. Some stayed
and so shared whatever apartment, food, bed, clothes that
were available. We stopped being guests at each other's
houses and no longer felt the need to entertain or be enter-
taining. Kitchens became liberated territory. Women still did

Excerpted from Marty Jezer, "How I Came Here," in *Home Comfort: Stories and Scenes
of Life on Total Loss Farm*, edited by Richard Wizansky. Reprinted with permission from
Marty Jezer.

most of the cleaning and the cooking (that would become an issue later), but we stopped thinking of our little apartments as *ours*. All kinds of people, some whom I didn't know, lived in my apartment. . . . What a pleasure it was to live in New York those days. There were four or five apartments scattered throughout the city where I could spend time, eat, sleep, and feel at home.

Slowly, we were becoming a family. We weren't aware of the process, one step suggested a next step and circumstances dictated the direction. In the spring of 1967 the Beatles' *Sergeant Pepper* album came out. I remember doing little else during the evenings of that best of all summers but visiting with friends and listening to Sergeant Pepper, stoned and silent. Sergeant Pepper was our catechism. The Beatles gave us the words to describe our feelings. "It's getting better all the time" and "I get by with a little help from my friends. " The world seemed to be coming apart all around us; yet in the growing hippie subculture we were experiencing an unprecedented ecstatic high. Our world, at least, was getting better all the time, and, if nothing else, we had our friends, which seemed more than enough. "With our love, we could save the world," we felt, "if they only knew" and, by God, we were more than ready to share in the good news. The *Win* [magazine] staff became the *Win* family, and with thousands of other small families scattered across the nation, one big spaced-out tribe.

The Movement Versus the Government

After that summer of love, the bubble that the Beatles had created burst. The pieces fell all around us but the vision that was at its heart remained as ever, dazzling and clear. The problem, we thought, was that we had created our beloved community in the eye of a hurricane and that the hurricane, which was the movement, was spiraling out of control toward a head-on confrontation with the government. The tension, obviously, helped bring us together. But the pressure was too great and the speed with which events were unfolding worked to drive us apart.

Between the Pentagon demonstration in October '67 and the Battle of Chicago [at the Democratic Convention] in August '68 we were in continuous confrontation with the police. Every weekend saw a different street action. Throwing money away at the stock exchange. Running through the street to declare "The War Is Over" as if the power of our self-prophecy could make a reality out of an illusion. The Resistance was at its peak with morning [Draft] induction refusals, picket lines and rallies, and Yippie was chipping away at the sanctity of the state through satire and obscenity. Demonstrations became social events, what one did every weekend. We lived from action to action, the weekly encounters with authority defined our lives. By the time Chicago came up, we were all tough battle-hardened veterans of a score and more skirmishes with the police. It dawned on some of us, too late I suppose, that we had entered into a cycle of escalation similar to the pattern of the war. The more disruptive we became, the more force the government would muster to keep us down. Our desperation seemed justified at the time, and I suppose, if it's any consolation, history will be kind. Our radical views about Vietnam and about our government, as events have proven, were in every respect right. Yet neither the press, the public, nor the government took us seriously. It seemed that trying to disrupt the orderly workings of society was the only thing left we could do.

The Violence of Our Own People

The desperation of the movement caused problems for those of us committed to nonviolence. We were advocates of disruption, of course; in fact, pioneers of the more gentle aspects of the art. But the threshold of anger had become so high that nonviolent action was no longer possible. As more and more movement people started to bait and then fight the police, the pacifists found themselves in the compromising position of trying to cool both sides out. Chicago was the last demonstration I've ever attended. I went, planning to write about it for *Liberation* Magazine. But I never wrote the article. I saw things happen in Chicago about which I didn't want to write. . . .

What frightened me at Chicago—and I wish I had had the courage to say it in 1968 (though no one would have been in a frame of mind to listen)—was the violence of our own people and the way it raged out of control. The few movement veterans who came to fight police and did so didn't bother me. They knew what they were doing and did as expected. It was the hippie kids who answered the call to a festival of life and the [Peace Candidate Eugene] McCarthy followers who came to Chicago still believing in the system. Overnight they were transformed into an angry and hateful mob without any political understanding of their violence except sweet and righteous revenge. You cannot build a movement for social change on the emotions of revenge. The turning point was 1968. Some of my friends became Weatherpeople [a terrorist faction of the Students for a Democratic Society]. Others disappeared into the woods. The peace movement had reached a dead end. There seemed to be no middle ground.

Chicago confirmed an earlier instinct that it was time to drop out. Earlier in the year, I went to Washington, D.C. , to help Ray Mungo on Liberation News Service. I first heard of Ray when he was editing the B.U. [Boston University] *News* and raising the same kind of hell in Boston that we were stirring up in New York. Since I had dropped out of B.U. grad school I wrote Ray a fan letter urging him to keep up the good fight. Ray, it turned out, was a fan of *Win,* so we continued our correspondence, which led, right in the middle of the riots after the death of Martin Luther King, Jr., to me going to Washington to lend a hand at LNS.

To Vermont to Buy a Farm

Two busts during the rioting—one for curfew, the other for dope—turned us instantly into old and trusting friends. I met [Commune partner] Verandah when she sat next to me during a double feature of the Marx Brothers' *Duck Soup* and a Mae West feature, title long forgotten. . . . I moved into the LNS communal pad on Church Street and staked my future on Ray and Verandah's gift for fantasy. It wasn't long before we were headed up to Vermont (after a brief detour to California) to buy a farm, of all things; but perhaps I should explain myself further.

By 1968 the *Win* family had pretty much burned itself out. . . . Politically, we had staked our pacifism on the success of The Resistance. We believed (and I still do) that if all the people who opposed the war had actively supported The Resistance (by turning in their draft cards and refusing induction if they were young males of draft age) we could have ended it. . . . But though many people gave lip-service support, relatively few people put their bodies on the line. A lot of our friends went to jail. I was lucky and never got indicted. But it didn't seem at the time that pacifism had anywhere to go, or at least I no longer felt I had anything original to contribute. So I needed to phase myself out of *Win*.

Yet, the experience at *Win* propelled me further in the direction I always seemed to be going. I didn't want to be just a writer, or just a person who functioned in some capacity in the movement. I wanted to build on the idea of community that had started to take shape at *Win*. That is, I wanted to start all over from scratch, reshape my own life and see how far a small group of people could take the idea of community together, hoping that out of the experience I'd have something later to write or offer the movement. Remember, we were all heavily into politics and committed to "making a revolution." I was very self-conscious about these motives. When Ray and Verandah had their fantasy about Vermont (and I never considered it more than fantasy at the beginning), I immediately agreed to go along. Though we only knew each other about a month, there was a lot of love, trust, and respect between us all. Those were fast-moving days and we all formed allegiances, made friendships, and fell in love on the basis of vibrations and elemental instincts. The fact that we got along and were headed in a common and communal direction was sufficient for each of us to commit whatever it was that shone dimly as our future to each other.

Go with the Flow

Well, one step led to another and much to my astonishment we were soon headed to Vermont to buy this farm which, somehow, Ray and Verandah knew about from this friend they had . . . I never quite understood the details. We looked at the farm, satisfied that it had a house on it, grass and trees (noting little else), and I met some of the other people who were going to live on the farm. Everyone seemed weird, but so was I and it seemed that if the farm was really going to happen I should go with the flow.

In June, 1968, we bought the farm. I assembled my life savings of $2,500, half of the necessary down payment, and threw it into a common pot. We signed the papers and I still had a hundred dollars left. Ray decided we needed to buy a car or maybe I heard wrong and he needed to buy a car. At any rate, I said "Far out," and with my last hundred dollars Ray bought an old Rambler sedan, which he named Nelly Belle, registered it to himself, and drove off to Washington, D.C., to close out his affairs. For a very brief instant I was stricken with an explosive flash of paranoia, a blast, I suppose, from my not quite forgotten straighter past. What in God's name had I gotten into? Here I'd invested every cent I had in a farm which we knew nothing about, with some crazy people who I hardly knew, and then Ray had taken my very last penny and absconded with what I believed was to be *our* car. But that feeling didn't last for long. Our lives, by then, had become structured on faith. If I couldn't trust my brother, who could I trust? The farm had to work out because I couldn't think of what I'd do next if it didn't. It was, as I said in the beginning, the end of the line. There was and is no place else to go.

As you can guess, everything did work out.

Chapter 4

Guerrilla Politics

Chapter Preface

In the early sixties, many men who marched in antiwar demonstrations wore suits and ties, women wore skirts and sweaters. This was done so as to not distract average Americans from the protesters' thoughtful message. When these protesters began taking LSD and were joined by thousands of wildly dressed hippies, the movement took on an entirely different tone of "us" versus "them."

The early cries for peace fell on deaf ears in Washington, and the protesters became increasingly angry as their demands went unanswered. In response, media-savvy leaders began to manipulate reporters. Instead of organizing huge demonstrations which were mostly ignored, activists like Abbie Hoffman and Jerry Rubin staged outrageous events—such as dumping hundreds of dollars onto the floor of the New York Stock Exchange—that were sure to attract the television cameras. The picture of hundreds of stock traders jumping over each other to grab a few dollar bills was worth a thousand words to millions of Americans who saw it on the evening news.

Hoffman and Rubin were founders of the Youth International Party, or Yippies, and both pioneers of this sort of media manipulation, concocting ridiculous episodes to shock America out of its complacency. Hoffman's book, *Revolution for the Hell of It,* and Rubin's book *Do It!* were the best-selling handbooks of the radical revolution. And the Yippies befriended John Lennon, leader of the Beatles, who could summon the world's top media in a matter of days to draw attention to his guerrilla politics version of peace and love.

The Birth of the Yippies

Jerry Rubin

There were many radical groups assembled at the 1968 Chicago convention, including the Youth International Party, or Yippies, who used outrageous media stunts to draw attention to the antiwar movement, including running a pig named Pigasus as their presidential candidate. The name and idea for the Yippies was conceived at a New Year's Eve party eight months earlier.

Jerry Rubin was one of the founders of the Yippies who used shock and humorous antics to protest the war. In the following excerpt from his book *Do It!* he explains the creation and ideology of the Yippies.

We got very stoned so we could look at the problem *logically*:

It's a *youth* revolution.

Gimme a "Y."

It's an *international* revolution.

Gimme an "I."

It's people trying to have meaning, fun, ecstasy in their lives—a *party*.

Gimme a "P."

Whattaya got?

Youth International Party.

[Author and activist] Paul Krassner jumped to his feet and shouted: *"YIP-pie! We're yippies!"*

A movement was born.

All of us in the room that New Year's Eve knew, when we heard it, that in a few months "yippie" would become a household word.

Abbie [and] Anita [Hoffman], Paul, Nancy [my girlfriend] and I began jumping up and down all around the room, yipping.

Would people really call themselves yippies?

A few months earlier [Secretary of State] Dean Rusk came to town and we ran through the streets setting fires in trash cans, splashing blood onto passing limousines and disrupting traffic. As we ran, we shouted something that sounded like "yippie."

Yippie is the sound of surging through the streets.

Yippies—the name of a nonorganization, nonpolitical party—the Youth International Party. Also the actor in the party: a yippie! And the battle cry: YIPPIE!

Myths offer kids a model to identify with.

Amerika's myths—from George Washington to Superman to Tarzan to John Wayne—are dead. Amerikan youth must create their own myths.

A Hybrid Mixture

A new man was born smoking pot while besieging the Pentagon, but there was no myth to describe him. There were no images to describe all the 14-year-old freeks in Kansas, dropping acid, growing their hair long and deserting their homes and their schools. There were no images to describe all the artists leaving the prison of middle-class Amerika to live and create art on the streets.

The Marxist acidhead, the psychedelic Bolshevik. He didn't feel at home in SDS, and he wasn't a flower-power hippie or a campus intellectual. A stoned politico. A hybrid mixture of New Left and hippie coming out something different.

A streetfighting freek, a dropout, who carries a gun at his hip. So ugly that middle-class society is frightened by how he looks.

A longhaired, bearded, hairy, crazy motherfucker whose life is theater, every moment creating the new society as he destroys the old.

The reality was there. A myth was needed to coalesce the energy.

Yippies forged that myth and inspired potential yippies in

The Yippie Manifesto

The Yippies had a long list of demands that included an end to the war in Vietnam and the elimination of money. Before the Democratic presidential convention in Chicago, Yippie leader Abbie Hoffman wrote a list of eighteen points in the Yippie political program which were printed on leaflets and distributed to protesters in the parks. Rather than put his name on the leaflet, Hoffman simply signed it "A. Yippie."

Revolution Towards a Free Society: Yippie!
By A. Yippie

This is a personal statement. There are no spokesmen for the Yippies . . . We are all our own leaders . . . We demand a society built along the alternative community in [Chicago's] Lincoln Park, a society based on humanitarian cooperation and equality, a society which allows and promotes the creativity present in all people and especially our youth.

1. An immediate end to the War in Vietnam and a restructuring of our foreign policy which totally eliminates aspects of military, economic, and cultural imperialism . . . and the abolition of the military draft.

2. Immediate freedom for Huey Newton of the Black Panthers and all other black people. . .

3. The legalization of marihuana and all other psychedelic drugs. The freeing of all prisoners currently in prison on narcotics charges. . .

5. A judicial system which works towards the abolition of all laws related to crimes without victims.

6. The total disarmament of all the people beginning with the police. This includes not only guns, but such brutal devices as tear gas, MACE, electric prods, blackjacks, billy clubs and the like.

every small town and city throughout the country to throw down their textbooks and be free.

Yippies would use the Democratic Party and the Chicago theater to build our stage and make the myth; we'd steal the

---

7. The Abolition of Money. The abolition of pay housing, pay media, pay transportation, pay food, pay education, pay clothing, pay medical help, and pay toilets.

8. A society which works toward and actively promotes the concept of "full-unemployment.". . . Adoption of the concept "Let the Machines do it."

9. A conservation program . . . committed to the elimination of pollution from our air and water. . .

12. A restructured educational system which provides the student power to determine his course of study and allows for student participation in over-all policy planning. . .

13. The open and free use of the media. A program which actively supports and promotes cable television as a method of increasing the selection of channels available to the viewer.

14. An end to all censorship. . .

15. We believe that people should fuck all the time, anytime, whomever they wish. This is not a program demand but a simple recognition of the reality around us.

16. A political system which is more . . . responsive to the needs of all the people regardless of age, sex or race. Perhaps a national referendum system conducted via television or a telephone voting system. Perhaps a decentralization of power . . . with many varied tribal groups. . .

17. A program that encourages and promotes the arts. However, we feel that if the Free Society we envision were to be fought for and achieved . . . we would have a society in which every man would be an artist. . .

It is for these reasons that we have come to Chicago [and] many of us may die here . . . Political Pigs, your days are numbered. We are the Second American Revolution. We shall win. Yippie!

Quoted in Larry Sloman, *Steal This Dream: Abbie Hoffman and the Counterculture Revolution in America.* New York: Doubleday, 1998.

media away from the Democrats and create the specter of "yippies" overthrowing Amerika.

The myth is real if it builds a stage for people to play out their own dreams and fantasies.

The myth is always bigger than the man. The myth of [Cuban Revolutionary] Che Guevara is even more powerful than Che. The myth of SDS [Students for a Democratic Society] is stronger than SDS.

The myth of yippie will overthrow the government.

The myth makes the revolution. Marx is a myth. Mao is a myth. [Bob] Dylan is a myth. The Black Panthers are a myth.

People try to fulfill the myth; it brings out the best in them.

"Abandon the Creeping Meatball"

The secret to the yippie myth is that it's nonsense. Its basic informational statement is a blank piece of paper.

The left immediately attacked us as apolitical, irrational, acidhead freeks who were channeling the "political rebellion of youth" into dope, rock music and be-ins. The hippies saw us as Marxists in psychedelic clothes using dope, rock music and be-ins to radicalize youth politically at the end of a policeman's club.

The hippies see us as politicos and the politicos see us as hippies. Only the right wing sees us for what we actually are.

The slogan of the yippies is: *"Rise up and abandon the creeping meatball!"* The straight press thought that "creeping meatball" meant [President] Lyndon Baines Johnson and that we wanted to throw him out of office.

We just laughed, because we love LBJ. LBJ was our leader, founder, guru. Where would we be without LBJ?

Everybody has his own creeping meatball—grades, debts, pimples. Yippies are a participatory movement. There are no ideological requirements to be a yippie. Write your own slogan. Protest your own issue. Each man his own yippie.

All you have to do to be a yippie is to be a yippie.

Yippie is just an excuse to rebel.

If you ask "Do yippies really exist?" then you're not a yippie.

If you say, "There are no yippies," you're not a yippie.

Last year's yippie is already respectable.

This year's yippie sucks.

Yippies are freaky so kids out there will say, "I can be freaky and get away with it, too."

When somebody gets further out than the yippies, then it's time to get further out than them, or dissolve the yippies.

Yippies believe there can be no social revolution without a head revolution and no head revolution without a social revolution.

Leaders Without Followers

There's no such thing as a YIPPIE FOLLOWER. There are 646½ million different kinds of yippies, and the definition of a yippie is that he is a LEADER. Yippies are *Leaders without followers*.

Yippies do whatever we want to do whenever we want to do it. Yippies know we're sane and everyone else is crazy, so we call ourselves "the crazies."

Yippies say if it's not fun, don't do it.

We see sex, rock 'n' roll and dope as part of a Communist plot to take over Amerika.

We cry when we laugh and laugh when we cry.

To be a yippie you got to watch color television at least two hours a day, especially the news.

The yippie idea of fun is overthrowing the government.

Yippies are Maoists.

Yippies are put-ons because we make our dreams public. . . .

Reporter: Where do the yippies get their money?

Yippie: Did you ever ask the Pope where he got his ring?

Nothing to Lose

Yippies are city freeks. We feel at home in a traffic jam.

The left demands full employment for all—we demand full unemployment for all. The world owes us a living!

Straights shit in their pants when they hear the yippies reveal the most crucial political issue in Amerika today: pay toilets.

Yippies want to run naked through the halls of Congress.

The yippies hold secret strategy meetings with [California Governor] Ronnie Reagan to plan how to radicalize Berkeley students.

Yippies get stoned on Fidel's speeches.

We started yippie with an office, a mailing list, three telephone lines, five paid staff organizers, weekly general meetings and weekly Steering Committee meetings. We were the hardest workers and most disciplined people you ever met, even though we extol sloth and lack of discipline. We are a living contradiction, because we're yippies.

Marijuana is compulsory at all yippie meetings.

Yippies take acid at breakfast to bring us closer to reality. . . .

Yippies believe every nonyippie is a repressed yippie. We try to bring out the yippie in everybody.

Yippies proclaim: *Straights of the world, drop out*! *You have nothing to lose but your starched shirts*!

The revolution will come when everybody is a Yippie!

Abbie Hoffman Raises the Pentagon

Abbie Hoffman

Abbie Hoffman was known for his ability to shock America with ridiculous, humorous, and absurd antics which were always widely covered by the media. In 1967 Hoffman organized a huge rally at the Pentagon in Washington, D.C.

The stated purpose of Hoffman's rally was to cast the evil spirits from the the massive, five-sided home office of the United States military by raising it five feet in the air through the use of group psychic powers. In the weeks before the event, Hoffman and his companions staged a media blitz to announce to America the promise of a levitated Pentagon.

Abbie Hoffman began his political activism working with the civil rights organization, SNCC (Student Nonviolent Coordinating Committee). He was one of the founders of the loosely organized Yippie movement in 1966 which coordinated dozens of major protests. In the late sixties and early seventies Hoffman's books, *Revolution for the Hell of It,* *Woodstock Nation,* and *Steal This Book,* were all bestsellers. Hoffman went into hiding in 1974 after he was arrested for cocaine possession, finally surrendering to authorities in 1980. After two years in prison, Hoffman continued as an activist for peace and environmental causes. The Yippie leader died in his home in Pennsylvania in 1989. Although some of his followers believe he was murdered by shadowy government figures, Hoffman's death was ruled a suicide.

Excerpted from Abbie Hoffman, *Soon to Be a Major Motion Picture.* Reprinted with permission from Elaine Markson Literary Agency.

All [Resisters] . . . must employ a certain element of magic if their battles are to be successful. Spiritual purification is sought as an antidote to the demons present in all imperialist war machines. On October 21, in the year 19 and 67, we would launch our holy crusade to cast forth the evil spirits dwelling in the Pentagon. It was written in the books of several religions that five-sided figures were devil-created. No one who read the fine print of *The New York Times* doubted that Vietnam War policy was the creation of Lucifer. What should one make of cluster bombs—that open a hundred meters above the ground, releasing bomblets which in turn release a spray of deadly needles killing all that is human in their wake? Silent penetration of body flesh. Can one talk in civil terms about saturation bombings, strategic hamlets, and free-fire zones? Could you describe napalm to a ten-year-old? Dropped in large barrels, a jelly-gas that spread rapidly through villages and stuck to the skin with a fiery grip. Or herbicidal defoliants designed to poison miles upon miles of plants and trees. Not since the Romans, in revenge, salted the earth of Carthage, has the world seen such a calculated wasteland. And the enemy? The "gooks" our young boys were commanded to kill in order to preserve the American Way of Life? Is there anyone now who believes God and napalm could ever end up on the same side?

Speaking to the Vietnamese

I knew the U. S. was not to triumph in the war on the day a wise Vietnamese colonel named Xuan Oanh (pronounced "wineown") told me the following:

> You must come to realize how we Vietnamese relate to the war. Many of us had never seen an airplane before. In the mountains and jungles the people believed they were flying dragons, dropping fire-eggs on their villages. The fear is beyond comprehension to Westerners. We trained villagers not to be afraid. Farmers learned to stand in their fields and shoot rifles at jet planes. Several times they would be successful. It would be foolhardy to dismiss supernatural forces as allies.

Xuan Oanh was an extraordinary warrior. A superior jungle fighter, he could also don the diplomat's garb when it became necessary to negotiate with [Secretary of State Henry] Kissinger in Paris. In his mid-fifties, though he looked twenty-eight, Xuan, a soldier for some forty years, remained a man of peace. He was the counterculture's man in Hanoi, in Paris, and in the tunnels and trenches of South Vietnam. Lacking formal education, he nonetheless managed to speak five languages fluently. Though he never mentioned it, many in his family had been tortured by Saigon intelligence officers trying to track him. His evasive tactics were legendary. Once when I saw him in Paris, he mentioned he was going home. "How do you go back, Xuan?" I queried. "I fly by commercial airline to Moscow, then transfer to a fighter jet headed to Hanoi. That takes about sixteen hours, then I walk home. That part takes six months." Knowing the magic of time travel, he could adapt to all the world's jungles. He also had an uncanny ability to begin conversation on exactly the right note. Once during a visit, after Woodstock, he asked [my wife] Anita if she could send him a Janis Joplin record. Later, in exchange, he presented her with a hash pipe fashioned from the metal wing of a felled jet plane. "Amazing," she exclaimed on the taxi ride from the embassy, "I swear he read my mind. He knew I had run out of rolling papers."

Needless to say, we had a different view of the Vietnamese than did the Pentagon. Coming out of Buddhist culture, they understood the significance of American martyrs dousing themselves in gasoline and torching their bodies in protest. They would not dismiss as frivolous attempts to exorcise the Pentagon. To the contrary, this was one conspiracy that actually could have hatched in Hanoi. Without saying a word, Xuan Oanh could easily let us entertain the illusion the idea was our own. Being young and hungry, we acted on that illusion. What the heck!

Measuring the Pentagon

Marty Carey and I began the ritual by standing in no-trespassing territory on the lawn surrounding one flank of the granite beast [the Pentagon]. (Just in case you have trouble distinguishing guerrilla leadership from an imperialist high command, consider the headquarters of the National Liberation Front [the Viet Cong]—a floating collective moving by night from hand-dug jungle tunnels to secret back rooms inside Saigon. The U.S. forces, on the other hand, were directed from the world's largest office building.) Marty brought some incense and Tibetan bells, we improvised an Apache war dance and proceeded to measure at arm's length the distance from one corner to the next. "What the hell is going on here?" screamed the M.P. sergeant, racing up to us with bayonet poised. Paying no attention, we continued.

"One hundred and one, one hundred and two, one hundred and three. . . ," we counted, exchanging positions with each number. Soon there was a circle of concerned officials. Braided uniforms signifying Army brass. Suit-and-tie costumes of public-relations men. "Just what's going on here?" asked a uniform.

"Well, *corporal*, as you know, five-sided objects are evil. We're here to begin the exorcism of the Pentagon," said Abbie.

"Now wait a minute. This is government property, and it's *captain*."

"We'll be done soon," explained Marty. "We just have to measure one side and multiply by five. We have to see how many witches we need to circle the Pentagon. "

"Circle the Pentagon? Sergeant, what in God's name is going on here?" shouted the captain.

"Exactly," responded Marty. "See, as part of the levitation ceremony. . . "

"Levitation!" he exploded.

"Don't worry, general, we're applying for a permit. We want permission to raise the Pentagon one hundred feet," continued Marty.

"It'll all be legal," I added in a responsible tone.

"Goddamn it, sergeant, arrest these lunatics!"

The arrest created national interest. "We'll be back with fifty thousand more next month," we announced.

"Did you get the permit?" inquired the press.

"We are negotiating permission to raise this hunk of granite one hundred feet, the generals so far agree to only ten. We're reasonable, ten feet will have to do. See you next month, boys and girls."

Guerrilla Theater

Witches were recruited . . . costumed appropriately, and sent on TV talk shows to entertain and inform the people of our plans. Hildi Hoffman, chief witch of the Group Image, baffled one host when she poured red sand on his studio floor, drew a pentagon figure with a stick, and starting weirding out on incantations. We constructed a huge plywood replica of the Potomac monster, and at a dress rehearsal on the stage of the Fillmore East [concert hall] managed to get the bugger to rise. It took [rock group] Fugs, music, smoke bombs, and a network of thin piano wires slung over the rafters.

When the Washington police announced they were prepared to use the dreaded mace spray to blind demonstrators, we announced that our scientists had invented a new drug called—"Lace." "Lace is LSD combined with DMSO, a skin-penetrating agent. When squirted on the skin or clothes, it penetrates quickly to the bloodstream, causing the subject to disrobe and get sexually aroused," I announced to a bewildered but horny press. For the few cynical holdouts we staged an orgy. Water pistols were loaded with the secret Lace which had been smuggled into the U. S. from Taiwan in plastic containers labeled "Schwartz Disappear-O!" Marketed as a novelty item, it appeared to cause a purple stain, then vanished before your eyes. Magic!

I called some reporters and told them we had a new drug that made people want to fuck. "How do we know it's true?" they said. I told them to come over to the house for a demonstration. They all showed up, and we ushered them into a room we had set up with pillows on the floor, assembling the reporters against the wall and introducing them to the two couples who were to demonstrate the effects of Lace. I gave a little speech full of mumbo-jumbo about the new drug, cautioning them not to touch the containers as the stuff hadn't been tested yet.

After my speech, I had to slip out to speak at a church. Having no idea the couples were going to go all the way, so to speak, for the revolution, I'm annoyed to this day that I missed the orgy. The subjects shot themselves with water pistols full of purple Lace, took off their clothes, and fucked. Then they put their clothes back on, and the reporters interviewed them. "What did it feel like?" they asked.

"Well, after about five minutes I began to see all sorts of colors . . ." Their answers were merely recollections of past acid experiences.

Within no time at all Johnny Carson was talking about the new and potent sex drug, Lace. At the time there was a lot of scare talk about drugs—LSD, mushrooms, STP, and Morning Glory seed—there were many new names floating around and a lot of stories that usually involved dopers doing bizarre things. People suspected the Lace demonstration was a put-on, but then again. . . . Hippies, drugs, orgies: it was all perfectly believable. A good joke and a good ad for the march on the Pentagon. Whatever terror ploy the Washington cops could dream up, we could top.

Flower Bombs

So two truckloads of Disappear-O!, water pistols, smoke bombs, Halloween masks, and noisemakers went south and were distributed just before dawn on the banks of the Potomac. One hour later, word came that one of our secret battalions, led by Walter Bowart, had been arrested at the airport. Busted with them were ten thousand flowers. They were nabbed boarding a small Piper Cub which was to penetrate the artillery defenses and flower-bomb the Pentagon with lilies. Some rat-fink had snitched the plot before the plane had a chance to challenge the radar.

Caravans of demonstrators began arriving from all over the country. At noon we assembled in front of the statue of Honest Abe Lincoln. It was warm for an October day, and young people stripped and swam nude in the reflecting pool. [A Yippie named] Radio Bob got into an early altercation with some Nazi hecklers and was hauled off to prison in a makeshift jail somewhere below the Washington Monument. . . . Thousands, more than a hundred thousand in all, turned out. The air rang with anticipation as the crowd heated up to the speeches and singing.

Then Dave Dellinger announced the ground rules: "No pushing, no shoving, no *violencia*; but those who so desire should now proceed to the walls of the Pentagon for civil disobedience." "Hup-Two-Three-Four, what the fuck are we fightin' for!" The war was about to come home. Welcome sisters and brothers to the Second American Revolution!

"To the Walls"

"Out demons out! Out demons out!" The chanting grew louder. [The rock group] Fugs and medicine men on flatbed trucks filled the air with the sounds of tambourines, drums, and screaming incantations. Anita, dressed as Sergeant Pepper, and myself, as an Indian with an Uncle Sam hat, held hands. We split our last tab of acid, hurtled the highway barrier wall, raced across the traffic, and scampered up the embankment. From there we could see the five-sided hulk stretched against the Virginia horizon. To the left and right were flanks of demonstrators crawling up the slope. Several carried Viet Cong flags. College pennants fluttered alongside banners proclaiming antiwar slogans. M.P.s in white helmets chased stragglers who raced through the highway traffic and disappeared into the bushes. Once on the top of the plateau, the plain ahead was flat, and the Pentagon was clearly visible. Helicopters whirled overhead. Thousands spread out in formation. "CHARGE!" I screamed at the top of my lungs, lunging forward. "To the walls! To the walls!" Adrenaline shot through the crowd's bloodstream. A swarm, fifty thousand strong, raced across the grass and hurled itself as one mighty mudball against the Pentagon. Dancing and cursing, we tried to encircle the joint. Between the building and us were platoons of soldiers, rifles and bayonets outstretched in menacing formation. A hush came over the crowd, instant leaders urged the people to sit down and be calm. The singing began:

> I lay down my sword and shield, down by the riverside,
> Down by the riverside, down by the riverside.
> I lay down my sword and shield, down by the riverside,
> Ain't gonna study war no more. . . .

Like a Flying Saucer

Super Joel, one of Berkeley's best street people, walked up to the bayonets and, in a gesture of courage and love, inserted a flower into a soldier's rifle barrel. It has remained one of the classic photos of the sixties.

Hours passed. Graffiti covered the outer barrier walls. HO CHI MINH LOVES LBJ, END WAR! THE NLF IS GONNA WIN, GUMBO WAS HERE. "Beat Army! Beat Army!"

Night came. Fires were lit to keep warm. People huddled under blankets. It was Valley Forge revisited. When the TV camera-eye could no longer see, the order went out and heads were busted. Some people fought back. Rumors flew. "Soldiers are deserting!" "Someone got shot!" Helicopters with spotlights hovered in the darkness, eerie reminders of Vietnam. The breath froze in the chilly autumn air as we scrambled on the ground to keep our hard-won turf. Paddy wagons and ambulances moved into position as the long tedious ritual of dragging people off to jail began.

Just before dawn, eleven of us assembled at the west wall. Our bellies ached from hunger, our fingers were stiff from the frost, paint and mascara streaked down our faces. The acid had long since worn off, leaving parched throats and lips begging for Chapstick. A Shoshone medicine man asked Anita to sit cross-legged facing the sun and lead us in prayer. Spontaneously an undulating sound arose from our circle of comrades. It was not unlike the battle cry of Algerian women. Words that shall remain secret were spoken by the shaman. Then Anita rose tall and proud, and in a voice possessed roared: OM AH HUM. OM AH HUM. OM AH HUM. The ground beneath us vibrated. The granite walls began to glow, matching the orange of the new sun, and then, before our very eyes, without a sound, the entire Pentagon rose like a flying saucer in the air.

What impressed me the most was the ease with which it happened. Child's play really. Of course, to "see" the levitation you had to be there that moment. Even being there in the physical sense was not enough, one had to master Don Juan's technique of *not-doing*—one had to learn how to stop the world. Xuan Oanh told me he had felt the Pentagon move while walking along the Ho Chi Minh Trail on his way home.

Quite apart from the metaphysics, the sight of the most famous war-making symbol on the planet under siege by thousands of its citizens was instantaneously transmitted around the globe. That needed no interpreter, no hocus-pocus.

Released from the D.C. jails, we headed back to our local communities: Madison, Atlanta, Ann Arbor, Berkeley, New Orleans, the Lower East Side. We already knew our next national rendezvous. In eight months we would reconvene outside the gates of the Democratic Convention. The location had no sooner been announced than we made our intentions clear. We would bring the war home to Chicago. Confidence high. Experience and courage already tested. We would stalk Lyndon Johnson as he campaigned throughout the land, building armies of protesters who would then flock to the Midwest and confront the policy makers with their own madness.

Radical Feminist Politics

Valerie Solanas

Although the guerrilla politics of the 1960s were dominated by men, a few women were not satisfied by the mainstream women's movement, and subscribed to extremely radical feminist beliefs. Probably the most radical of all were the members of the Society for Cutting Up Men (SCUM), who advocated the virtual murder of all males in society.

Valerie Solanas was sexually molested and abused as a young child and became a prostitute in the early 1960s. She wrote an obscene play that she tried to sell to avant-garde artist Andy Warhol in 1967. The same year she published the S.C.U.M. Manifesto—paraphrased below—which she sold on New York street corners. The 11,000-word manifesto is a scathing indictment of men's behavior in social, professional, and sexual situations. Laced with obscenities, the tract calls on women to seize all means of power in society and for men to commit suicide or be killed by women.

In 1968, Solanas shot and seriously wounded Warhol. Solanas received a short sentence for attempted murder. The incident was immortalized in the 1991 movie "I Shot Andy Warhol." Solanas lived the last years of her life as a drug-addicted prostitute in San Francisco, dying in 1988.

Life in this society being, at best, an utter bore and no aspect of society being at all relevant to women, there remains to civic-minded, responsible, thrill-seeking females

Excerpted from Valerie Solanas, *S.C.U.M. Manifesto.*

only to overthrow the government, eliminate the money system, institute complete automation and destroy the male sex.

It is now technically feasible to reproduce without the aid of males (or, for that matter, females) and to produce only females. We must begin immediately to do so. Retaining the male has not even the dubious purpose of reproduction. The male is a biological accident: the Y (male) gene is an incomplete X (female) gene, that is, it has an incomplete set of chromosomes. . . . To be male is to be deficient, emotionally limited; maleness is a deficiency disease and males are emotional cripples.

The male is completely egocentric, trapped inside himself, incapable of empathizing or identifying with others, or love, friendship, affection or tenderness. He is a completely isolated unit, incapable of rapport with anyone. His responses are entirely visceral, not cerebral; his intelligence is a mere tool in the services of his drives and needs; he is incapable of mental passion, mental interaction; he can't relate to anything other than his own physical sensations. He is a half-dead, unresponsive lump, incapable of giving or receiving pleasure or happiness; consequently, he is at best an utter bore, an inoffensive blob, since only those capable of absorption in others can be charming. He is trapped in a twilight zone halfway between humans and apes, and is far worse off than the apes because, unlike the apes, he is capable of a large array of negative feelings—hate, jealousy, contempt, disgust, guilt, shame, doubt—and moreover, he is aware of what he is and what he isn't.

Eaten Up with Guilt, Shame, and Insecurity

Although completely physical, the male is unfit even for stud service. Even assuming mechanical proficiency, which few men have, he is, first of all, incapable of zestfully, lustfully, [having sex], but instead is eaten up with guilt, shame, fear and insecurity, feelings rooted in male nature, which the most enlightened training can only minimize; second, the physical feeling he attains is next to nothing; and third, he is not empathizing with his partner, but is obsessed with how he's doing, turning in an "A" performance, doing a good plumbing job. To call a man an animal is to flatter him; he's a machine. . . . It's often said that men use women. Use them for what? Surely not pleasure. . . .

Being an incomplete female, the male spends his life attempting to complete himself, to become female. He attempts to do this by constantly seeking out, fraternizing with and trying to live through and fuse with the female, and by claiming as his own all female characteristics—emotional strength and independence, forcefulness, dynamism, decisiveness, coolness, objectivity, assertiveness, courage, integrity, vitality, intensity, depth of character, grooviness, etc.—and projecting onto women all male traits—vanity, frivolity, triviality, weakness, etc. It should be said, though, that the male has one glaring area of superiority over the female—public relations. . . . The male claim that females find fulfillment through motherhood and sexuality reflects what males think they'd find fulfilling if they were female. . . .

Niceness, Politeness, and 'Dignity': Every man, deep down, knows he's . . . worthless. Overwhelmed by a sense of animalism and deeply ashamed of it; wanting, not to express himself, but to hide from others his total physicality, total egocentricity, the hate and contempt he feels for other men, and to hide from himself the hate and contempt he suspects other men feel for him; having a crudely constructed nervous system that is easily upset by the least display of emotion or feeling, the male tries to enforce a 'social' code that ensures perfect blandness, unsullied by the slightest trace or feeling or upsetting opinion. . . .

Wanting to Maintain the System

Money, Marriage and Prostitution, Work and Prevention of an Automated Society: There is no human reason for money or for anyone to work more than two or three hours a week at the very most. All non-creative jobs (practically all jobs now being done) could have been automated long ago, and in a moneyless society everyone can have as much of the best of everything as she wants. But there are non-human, male reasons for wanting to maintain the money system:

1. Despising his highly inadequate self, overcome with intense anxiety and a deep, profound loneliness when by his empty self, desperate to attach himself to any female in dim hopes of completing himself, in the mystical belief that by touching gold he'll turn to gold, the male craves the continuous companionship of women. The company of the lowest female is preferable to his own or that of other men, who serve only to remind him of his repulsiveness. But females, unless very young or very sick, must be coerced or bribed into male company.

2. Supply the non-relating male with the delusion of usefulness, and enable him to try to justify his existence by digging holes and then filling them up. Leisure time horrifies the male, who will have nothing to do but contemplate his grotesque self. Unable to relate or to love, the male must work. Females crave absorbing, emotionally satisfying, meaningful activity, but lacking the opportunity or ability for this, they prefer to idle and waste away their time in ways of their own choosing—sleeping, shopping, bowling, shooting pool, playing cards and other games, breeding, reading, walking around, daydreaming, eating. . . gardening, sewing, nightclubbing, dancing, visiting, 'improving their minds' (taking courses), and absorbing 'culture' (lectures, plays, concerts, 'arty' movies). Therefore, many females would, even assuming complete economic equality between the sexes, prefer living with males or peddling their asses on the street, thus having most of their time for themselves, to spending many hours of their days doing boring, stultifying, non-creative work for someone else, functioning as less than animals, as machines. . . . What will liberate women, therefore, from male control is the total elimination of the money-work system, not the attainment of economic equality with men within it.

3. Power and control. Unmasterful in his personal relations with women, the male attains to masterfulness by the manipulation of money and everything controlled by money, in other words, of everything and everybody.

4. Love substitute. Unable to give love or affection, the male gives money. It makes him feel motherly. The mother gives milk; he gives bread. He is the Breadwinner.

5. Provide the male with a goal. Incapable of enjoying the moment, the male needs something to look forward to, and money provides him with an eternal, never-ending goal: Just think of what you could do with 80 trillion dollars—invest it! And in three years time you'd have 300 trillion dollars!!!

6. Provide the basis for the male's major opportunity to control and manipulate—fatherhood.

Daddy Wants What's Best for Daddy

Fatherhood and Mental Illness (fear, cowardice, timidity, humility, insecurity, passivity): Mother wants what's best for her kids; Daddy only wants what's best for Daddy, that is peace and quiet, pandering to his delusion of dignity ('respect'), a good reflection on himself (status) and the opportunity to control and manipulate, or, if he's an enlightened father, to 'give guidance'. . . . Daddy doesn't love his kids; he approves of them—if they're 'good', that is, if they're nice, 'respectful', obedient, subservient to his will, quiet and not given to unseemly displays of temper that would be most upsetting to Daddy's easily disturbed male nervous system—in other words, if they're passive vegetables. . . .

The effect of fatherhood on females is to make them male—dependent, passive, domestic, animalistic, insecure, approval and security seekers, cowardly, humble, 'respectful' of authorities and men, closed, not fully responsive, half-dead, trivial, dull, conventional, flattened-out and thoroughly contemptible. Daddy's Girl, always tense and fearful, uncool, unanalytical, lacking objectivity, appraises Daddy, and thereafter, other men, against a background of fear ('respect') and is not only unable to see the empty shell behind the facade, but accepts the male definition of himself as superior, as a female, and of herself, as inferior, as a male, which, thanks to Daddy, she really is. . . .

Prevention of Privacy: Although the male, being ashamed of what he is and almost of everything he does, insists on privacy and secrecy in all aspects of his life, he has no real regard for privacy. . . . Wanting to become a woman, he strives to be constantly around females, which is the closest he can get to becoming one, so he created a 'society' based upon the family. . . .

Conformity: Although he wants to be an individual, the male is scared of anything in himself that is the slightest bit different from other men, it causes him to suspect that he's not really a 'Man'. . . . So he tries to affirm his 'Manhood' by being like all the other men. . . .

Authority and Government: Having no sense of right and wrong, no conscience, which can only stem from having an ability to empathize with others . . . having no faith in his non-existent self, being unnecessarily competitive, and by nature, unable to co-operate, the male feels a need for external guidance and control. So he created authorities— priests, experts, bosses, leaders, etc.—and government. . . .

There's no reason why a society consisting of rational beings capable of empathizing with each other, complete and having no natural reason to compete, should have a government, laws or leaders. . . .

Competition, Prestige, Status, Formal Education, Ignorance and Social and Economic Classes: Having an obsessive desire to be admired by women, but no intrinsic worth, the male constructs a highly artificial society enabling him to appropriate the appearance of worth through money, prestige, 'high' social class, degrees, professional position and knowledge and, by pushing as many other men as possible down professionally, socially, economically, and educationally. . . .

Prevention of Conversation: Being completely self-centered and unable to relate to anything outside himself, the male's 'conversation', when not about himself, is an impersonal droning on, removed from anything of human value. Male 'intellectual conversation' is a strained compulsive attempt to impress the female. . . .

Eventually the natural course of events, of social evolution, will lead to total female control of the world and, subsequently, to the cessation of the production of males and, ultimately, to the cessation of the production of females.

But SCUM is impatient; SCUM is not consoled by the thought that future generations will thrive; SCUM wants to grab some thrilling living for itself. And, if a large majority of women were SCUM, they could acquire complete control of this country within a few weeks simply by withdrawing from the labor force, thereby paralyzing the entire nation. Additional measures, any one of which would be sufficient to completely disrupt the economy and everything else, would be for women to declare themselves off the money system, stop buying, just loot and simply refuse to obey all laws they don't care to obey. The police force, National Guard, Army, Navy and Marines combined couldn't squelch a rebellion of over half the population, particularly when it's made up of people they are utterly helpless without.

If all women simply left men, refused to have anything to do with any of them—ever, all men, the government, and the national economy would collapse completely. Even without leaving men, women who are aware of the extent of their superiority to and power over men, could acquire complete control over everything within a few weeks, could effect a total submission of males to females. In a sane society the male would trot along obediently after the female. The male is docile and easily led, easily subjected to the domination of any female who cares to dominate him. The male, in fact, wants desperately to be led by females, wants Mama in charge, wants to abandon himself to her care. But this is not a sane society, and most women are not even dimly aware of where they're at in relation to men.

The conflict, therefore, is not between females and males, but between SCUM—dominant, secure, self-confident, nasty, violent, selfish, independent, proud, thrill-seeking, free-wheeling, arrogant females, who consider themselves fit to rule the universe, who have free-wheeled to the limits of this 'society' and are ready to wheel on to something far beyond what it has to offer—and nice, passive, accepting 'cultivated', polite, dignified, subdued, dependent, scared, mindless, insecure, approval-seeking Daddy's Girls, who can't cope with the unknown, who want to hang back with the apes, who feel secure only with Big Daddy standing by, with a big strong man to lean on and with a fat, hairy face in the White House, who are too cowardly to face up to the hideous reality of what a man is, what Daddy is, who have cast their lot with the swine, who have adapted themselves to animalism, feel superficially comfortable with it and know no other way of 'life', who have reduced their minds, thoughts and sights to the male level, who, lacking sense, imagination and wit can have value only in a male 'society', who can have a place in the sun. . . .

Destroy All Useless Objects

But SCUM is too impatient to wait for the de-brainwashing of millions of assholes. Why should the swinging females continue to plod dismally along with the dull male ones? Why should the fates of the groovy and the creepy be inter-twined? Why should the active and imaginative consult the passive and dull on social policy? Why should the independent be confined to the sewer along with the dependent who need Daddy to cling to? A small handful of SCUM can take over the country within a year by systematically f—— up the system, selectively destroying property, and murder:

SCUM will become members of the unwork force. . . . For example, SCUM salesgirls will not charge for merchandise; SCUM telephone operators will not charge for calls; SCUM office and factory workers, . . . will secretly destroy equipment. SCUM will unwork at a job until fired, then get a new job to unwork at.

SCUM will forcibly relieve bus drivers, cab drivers and subway token sellers of their jobs and run buses and cabs and dispense free tokens to the public.

SCUM will destroy all useless and harmful objects—cars, store windows, 'Great Art', etc.

Eventually SCUM will take over the airwaves—radio and TV networks—by forcibly relieving of their jobs all radio and TV employees who would impede SCUM's entry into the broadcasting studios.

SCUM will couple-bust—barge into mixed (male-female) couples, wherever they are, and bust them up. . . .

Operate on a Criminal Basis

SCUM will always operate on a criminal as opposed to a civil disobedience basis, that is, as opposed to openly violating the law and going to jail in order to draw attention to an injustice. Such tactics acknowledge the rightness overall system and are used only to modify it slightly, change specific laws. SCUM is against the entire system, the very idea of law and government. SCUM is out to destroy the system, not attain certain rights within it. . . .

After the elimination of money . . . men will be stripped of the only power they have over psychologically independent females. They will be able to impose themselves only on the doormats, who like to be imposed on. The rest of the women will be busy solving the few remaining unsolved problems before planning their agenda for eternity and Utopia—completely revamping educational programs so that millions of women can be trained within a few months for high level intellectual work that now requires years of training (this can be done very easily once our educational goal is to educate and not perpetuate an academic and intellectual elite); solving the problems of disease and old age and death and completely redesigning our cities and living quarters. . . .

The sick, irrational men, those who attempt to defend themselves against their disgustingness, when they see SCUM barrelling down on them, will cling in terror to Big Mama . . . but [Mama] won't protect them against SCUM. . . . Men who are rational, however, won't kick or struggle or raise a distressing fuss, but will just sit back, relax, enjoy the show and ride the waves to their demise.

Rock and Roll for Peace

John Lennon, interviewed by Richie Yorke

Like Abbie Hoffman and Jerry Rubin, John Lennon, singer
and songwriter for the Beatles, recognized the power of the
media to further the cause of peace. In 1969 the Beatles were
the most popular band in the world and the press followed
their every move from the release of a new album to the marriage of John Lennon to Japanese avant-garde artist Yoko
Ono. Lennon and Ono used their popularity to stage a "Bed-
In for Peace," on their honeymoon in Amsterdam.

In early 1969, the couple decided to put together the
world's biggest rock festival in Canada featuring the Beatles,
Bob Dylan, and even Elvis Presley. The proceeds for this concert were to be donated to groups working for peace. The
logistical nightmare of arranging such a concert plus the lack
of support from the Canadian government put a quick end to
Lennon's plans. Instead, Lennon and Ono, at their own
expense, put up huge billboards in New York's Time Square
and twelve other large cities in the world that said, "War is
Over! If You Want It."

The following press conference, from June 28, 1969 was
given when Lennon still had hopes of arranging the mythical
concert. Richie Yorke who edited the interview wrote several
books about rock stars such as Led Zeppelin and Van Morrison. He worked with Lennon and Ono for the "War is Over!
If You Want It" peace campaign in 1969.

Excerpted from Richie Yorke, "The Press Conference," in *The Ballad of John and Yoko*,
edited by Jonathan Cott and Christina Doudna. Reprinted with permission from Ritchie
Yorke.

There are a lot of people around the world now trying to promote world peace. Why do you think that you can succeed where they have so far failed?

That's like saying why bother keeping on Christianity because Jesus got killed. We don't think people have tried advertising before. Pretend peace is new then 'cause we've never had it. So you start advertising it: . . . Sell, sell, sell. . . .

Was there any one incident that got you into the peace campaign?

Well, it built up over a number of years, but the thing that struck it off was a letter we got from a guy called Peter Watkins, who made a film called *The War Game.* It was a long letter stating what's happening—how the media is controlled, how it's all run, and it ended up: "What are you going to do about it?"

He said people in our position and his position have a responsibility to use the media for world peace. And we sat on the letter for three weeks and thought it over and figured at first we were doing our best with songs like "All You Need Is Love."

Finally we came up with the bed event and that was what sparked it off. It was like getting your call-up papers for peace. Then we did the bed event. . . .

You said you were going to have a peace vote. How do you answer accusations that that sort of thing borders on naiveté?

Let's see. If anybody thinks our campaign is naive, that's their opinion and that's okay. Let them do something else and if we like their ideas, we'll join in with them. But until then, we'll do it the way we are. We're artists, not politicians. Not newspapermen, not anything. We do it in the way that suits us best, and this is the way we work.

Publicity and things like that is our game. The Beatles' thing was that. And that was the trade I've learned. This is my trade, and I'm using it to the best of my ability.

But what is the point of having a vote for peace?

Why do people have those Gallup polls? If we get a vote from around the world with millions and millions of kids that want peace, that's a nice Gallup poll. We can wave those figures around. That's all. It's a positive move; all we want is a yes. . . .

Vote for Peace

How soon can, the world reach a state of peace?

As soon as people realize that they have the power. The power doesn't belong with [Canadian Prime Minister] Mr. Trudeau, [English Prime Minister] Mr. Wilson or Mr. Nixon. We are the power. The people are the power. And as soon as people are aware that they have the power, then they can do what they want. And if it's a case of they don't know what to do, let's advertise to them to tell them they have an option. They've all got a vote. Vote for peace, folks.

Don't you think your long hair and your clothes may put old people off in your pursuit of peace?

I understand that. Many people say, "Why don't you get a butch haircut and a tie, suit?" and the thing is, that's what politicians do. We just try to be as natural as possible. Now, how many members of the public are gullible to politicians, with the nice picture of the family, the dog and the whore on the side? Now, I could do that, but I don't think people would believe it. That's the politicians' way, but youth certainly doesn't believe it anymore.

Have you ever thought of taking your ideas to someone like Henry Ford [Chairman of Ford Motor Co.]?

When we get a bit organized. You see, what we didn't want to become was leaders. I believe in [Austrian Psychoanalyst] Wilhelm Reich . . . who said, "Don't become a leader." We don't want to be the people that everyone says, "It was your fault we didn't get peace." We want to be part of it. It's like people said the Beatles were the movement; but we were only part of the movement. We were influenced as much as we influenced.

And John and Yoko refuse to be the leaders of the youth movement for peace. That's dictatorship. We want everybody to help us. And then, if it takes time for this kind of news to get through to Henry Ford . . . or anybody like that.

When we get something functional happening and a few

people that aren't John and Yoko, we can approach from that
angle. We can then say we've got so much money, will you
double it? 'Cause we know they all do charity for whatever
reason.

Everybody Is a Leader

Do you believe in God?

Yes, I believe that God is like a powerhouse, like where
you keep electricity, like a power station. And that he's a
supreme power, and that he's neither good nor bad, left, right,
black or white. He just is. And we tap that source of power
and make of it what we will. Just as electricity can kill people
in a chair, or you can light a room with it. I think God is.

Don't you worry about being identified as a father figure?

I believe that leaders and father figures are the mistake of
all the generations before us. And that all of us rely on
Nixon or Jesus or whoever we rely on; it's lack of responsibility that you expect somebody else to do it. He must help
me or we kill him or we vote him out. I think that's the mistake, just having father figures. It's a sign of weakness; you
must do the greasing yourself.

I won't be a leader. Everybody is a leader. People thought
the Beatles were leaders, but they weren't, and now people
are finding that out.

What, in brief, is your philosophy?

Peace, just no violence, and everybody grooving, if you
don't mind the word. Of course, we all have violence in us,
but it must be channeled or something. If I have long hair, I
don't see why everybody else should have long hair. And if
I want peace, I'll suggest peace to everyone. But I won't
hustle them up for peace.

If people want to be violent, let them not interfere with
people who don't want violence. Let them kill each other if
there has to be that.

Are there any alternatives?

You either get tired fighting for peace, or you die. . . .

*Getting back to how it started, how did you and Yoko ini-
tially find ground for this campaign?*

Both Yoko and I were in different bags, as we call it. But both had a positive side—we were singing "All You Need Is Love" and she was in Trafalgar Square, protesting for peace in a black bag. We met, we had to decide what our common goal was, we had one thing in common—we were in love. But love is just a gift, and it doesn't answer everything and it's like a precious plant that you have to nurture and look after and all that.

So we had to find what we wanted to do together—these two egos. What they had in common was love; we had to work on it. What goes with love, we thought, was peace. Now we were thinking of all this, and planning on getting married and not getting married and what we were going to do and how we were going to do it and rock & roll and avant-garde and all that bit, and then we got that letter from Peter Watkins. And it all started from there.

Chapter 5

Black Power

Chapter Preface

L ike the antiwar protesters, African American civil rights protests had started out peacefully. When Martin Luther King Jr. was met with police clubs and tear gas, he turned the other cheek, insisting that passive resistance would bring change. But just as the war protesters had become increasingly violent as their demands were ignored, by the late 1960s, many black people were tired of waiting for peaceful change, which was often promised but rarely delivered.

Black leaders such as Malcolm X began to advocate fighting back against white violence wherever it occurred. Malcolm X's words gave rise to the Black Power movement, whose members wanted equal rights immediately, and total black separation from white society.

After Malcolm X was murdered in 1965, other black voices joined in the chorus. Eldridge Cleaver, writing from prison, was not interested in sugar-coating the problems that existed for African Americans. He advocated the overthrow of the white power structure and a violent revolution among the repressed classes. Cleaver's words were celebrated by black radicals such as Bobby Seale and Huey Newton, who founded the Black Panther Party. The Panthers had little use for demonstrations and riots. They were armed and ready to fight the police just as people in Vietnam were fighting American soldiers.

As with the hippies and the Yippies this type of thinking was entirely new in America. Although many Panthers were eventually killed in shootouts with police or arrested, their fierce message of pride and resistance remains another part of the sixties counterculture that has integrated into today's society.

Malcolm X and Black Power

Malcolm X (as told to Alex Haley)

While civil rights leaders such as Martin Luther King Jr. preached peace and integration into white society, Malcolm X called for black power and racial separation. When Malcolm said that blacks had the right to fight racism with any means necessary—including violence—the press labeled him "America's angriest Negro." As an astute critic of white society, Malcolm's words formed the basis of the Black Power movement that shook the United States in the mid-1960s.

Malcolm X was the son of a Baptist minister who was allegedly killed by white supremacists. When his mother was committed to a mental institution several years later, Malcolm supported himself by stealing and selling drugs. After six years in prison, Malcolm became a member of the Nation of Islam, also known as the Black Muslims, eventually becoming the most famous spokesman for the group. In a battle over control of the organization, the 39-year-old X was gunned down at a rally in New York's Harlem on February 21, 1965 by three Nation of Islam assassins.

In the following excerpt, taken from his autobiography, Malcolm X explains why he is so angry at a white society that has oppressed his people for centuries.

L argely, the American white man's press refused to convey that I was now attempting to teach Negroes a new direction. With the 1964 "long, hot summer" steadily producing new incidents [of violence], I was constantly accused of "stirring up Negroes." Every time I had another radio or television microphone at my mouth. When I was asked about "stirring up Negroes" or "inciting violence," I'd get hot.

"It takes no one to stir up the sociological dynamite that stems from the unemployment, bad housing, and inferior education already in the ghettoes. This explosively criminal condition has existed for so long, it needs no fuse; it fuses itself; it spontaneously combusts from within itself. . . . "

They called me "the angriest Negro in America." I wouldn't deny that charge. I spoke exactly as I felt. "I *believe* in anger. The Bible says there is a *time* for anger." They called me "a teacher, a fomenter of violence." I would say point blank, "That is a lie. I'm not for wanton violence, I'm for justice. I feel that if white people were attacked by Negroes—if the forces of law prove unable, or inadequate, or reluctant to protect those whites from those Negroes—then those white people should protect and defend themselves from those Negroes, using arms if necessary. And I feel that, when the law fails to protect Negroes from whites' attack, then those Negroes should use arms, if necessary, to defend themselves."

Fight Against White Racists

"Malcolm X Advocates Armed Negroes!"

What was wrong with that? I'll tell you what was wrong. I was a black man talking about physical defense against the white man. The white man can lynch and burn and bomb and beat Negroes—that's all right: "Have patience". . . ."The customs are entrenched". . . "Things are getting better."

Well, I believe it's a crime for anyone who is being brutalized to continue to accept that brutality without doing something to defend himself. If that's how "Christian" philosophy is interpreted, if that's what [Indian leader Mahatma] Gandhian philosophy teaches, well, then, I will call them criminal philosophies.

I tried in every speech I made to clarify my new position regarding white people—"I don't speak against the sincere, well-meaning, good white people. I have learned that there *are* some. I have learned that not all white people are racists. I am speaking against and my fight is against the white *racists*. I firmly believe that Negroes have the right to fight against these racists, by any means that are necessary. "

But the white reporters kept wanting me linked with that word "violence." I doubt if I had one interview without having to deal with that accusation.

"I *am* for violence if non-violence means we continue postponing a solution to the American black man's problem—just to *avoid* violence. I don't go for non-violence if it also means a delayed solution. To me a delayed solution is a non-solution. Or I'll say it another way. If it must take violence to get the black man his human rights in this country, I'm *for* violence exactly as you know the Irish, the Poles, or Jews would be if they were flagrantly discriminated against. I am just as they would be in that case, and they would be for violence—no matter what the consequences, no matter who was hurt by the violence."

A Nation Born in Genocide

White society *hates* to hear anybody, especially a black man, talk about the crime the white man has perpetrated on the black man. I have always understood that's why I have been so frequently called "a revolutionist." It sounds as if *I* have done some crime! Well, it may be the American black man does need to become involved in a *real* revolution. The word for "revolution" in German is *Umwälzung*. What it means is a complete overturn—a complete change. . . . It means the destroying of an old system, and its replacement with a new system. . . . So how does anybody sound talking about the Negro in America waging some "revolution"? Yes, he is condemning a system—but he's not trying to overturn the system, or to destroy it. The Negro's so-called "revolt" is merely an asking to be *accepted* into the existing system! A *true* Negro revolt might entail, for instance, fighting for separate black states within this country—which several groups and individuals have advocated, long before [Black Muslim Leader] Elijah Muhammad came along.

When the white man came into this country, he certainly wasn't demonstrating any "non-violence." In fact, the very man whose name symbolizes non-violence here today has stated:

"Our nation was born in genocide when it embraced the doctrine that the original American, the Indian, was an inferior race. Even before there were large numbers of Negroes on our shores, the scar of racial hatred had already disfigured colonial society. From the sixteenth century forward, blood flowed in battles over racial supremacy. We are perhaps the only nation which tried as a matter of national policy to wipe out its indigenous population. Moreover, we elevated that tragic experience into a noble crusade. Indeed, even today we have not permitted ourselves to reject or to feel remorse for this shameful episode. Our literature, our films, our drama, our folklore all exalt it. Our children are still taught to respect the violence which reduced a red-skinned people of an earlier culture into a few fragmented groups herded into impoverished reservations."

Attracted by Spirit

"Peaceful coexistence!" That's another one the white man has always been quick to cry. Fine! But what have been the deeds of the white man? During his entire advance through history, he has been waving the banner of Christianity. . . and carrying in his other hand the sword and the flintlock.

You can go right back to the very beginning of Christianity, Catholicism, the genesis of Christianity as we know it to be presently constituted, with its hierarchy, was conceived in Africa—by those whom the Christian church calls "The Desert Fathers." The Christian church became infected with racism when it entered white Europe. The Christian church returned to Africa under the banner of the Cross—conquering, killing, exploiting, pillaging, raping, bullying, beating—and teaching white supremacy. This is how the white man thrust himself into the position of leadership of the world—through the use of naked physical power. And he was totally inadequate spiritually. Mankind's history has

Malcolm X addresses reporters' questions in 1964. The press labeled him "America's angriest Negro" because he advocated the use of violence in fighting racism.

proved from one era to another that the true criterion of leadership is spiritual. Men are attracted by spirit. By power, men are *forced*. Love is engendered by spirit. By power, anxieties are created.

I am in agreement one hundred percent with those racists who say that no government laws ever can *force* brotherhood. The only true world solution today is governments guided by true religion—of the spirit. Here in race-torn America, I am convinced that the Islam religion is desperately needed, particularly by the American black man. The black man needs to reflect that he has been America's most fervent Christian—and where has it gotten him? In fact, in the white man's hands, in the white man's interpretation . . . where has Christianity brought this *world*?

It has brought the non-white two-thirds of the human population to rebellion. Two-thirds of the human population today is telling the one-third minority white man, "Get out!" And the white man is leaving. And as he leaves, we see the non-white peoples returning in a rush to their original religions, which had been labeled "pagan" by the conquering white man. Only one religion—Islam—had the power to stand and fight the white man's Christianity for a *thousand years*! Only Islam could keep white Christianity at bay.

Reaping Racism

The Africans are returning to Islam and other indigenous religions. The Asians are returning to being Hindus, Buddhists and Muslims.

As the Christian Crusade once went East, now the Islamic Crusade is going West. With the East—Asia—closed to Christianity, with Africa rapidly being converted to Islam, with Europe rapidly becoming un-Christian, generally today it is accepted that the "Christian" civilization of America—which is propping up the white race around the world—is Christianity's remaining strongest bastion.

Well, if *this* is so—if the so-called "Christianity" now being practiced in America displays the best that world Christianity has left to offer—no one in his right mind should need any much greater proof that very close at hand is the *end* of Christianity.

Are you aware that some Protestant theologians, in their writings, are using the phrase "post-Christian era"—and they mean *now*?

And what is the greatest single reason for this Christian

church's failure? It is its failure to combat racism. It is the old "You sow, you reap" story. The Christian church sowed racism—blasphemously; now it reaps racism.

Sunday mornings in this year of grace 1965, imagine the "Christian conscience" of congregations guarded by deacons barring the door to black would-be worshipers, telling them "You can't enter *this* House of God!"

Tell me, if you can, a sadder irony than that St. Augustine, Florida—a city named for the black African saint who saved Catholicism from heresy—was recently the scene of bloody race riots.

I believe that God now is giving the world's so-called "Christian" white society its last opportunity to repent and atone for the crimes of exploiting and enslaving the world's non-white peoples. It is exactly as when God gave Pharaoh a chance to repent. But Pharaoh persisted in his refusal to give justice to those whom he oppressed. And, we know, God finally destroyed Pharaoh.

Is white America really sorry for her crimes against the black people? Does white America have the capacity to repent—and to atone? Does the capacity to repent, to atone, exist in a majority, in one-half, in even one-third of American white society?

Many black men, the victims—in fact most black men—would like to be able to forgive, to forget, the crimes.

But most American white people seem not to have it in them to make any serious atonement—to do justice to the black man.

Indeed, how *can* white society atone for enslaving, for raping, for unmanning, for otherwise brutalizing *millions* of human beings, for centuries? What atonement would the God of Justice demand for the robbery of the black people's labor, their lives, their true identities, their culture, their history—and even their human dignity?

A desegregated cup of coffee, a theater, public toilets—the whole range of hypocritical "integration"—these are not atonement.

Black Power and Law and Order

Eldridge Cleaver

Civil rights and racial equality had been promised to African Americans in the 1950s and early 1960s. In many big-city neighborhoods the words of the politicians rang hollow, and the promised changes had never materialized. Bad schools, poor housing, and lack of opportunity was causing a great seething anger among the black urban poor. In addition, police forces in inner-city neighborhoods were often 98 percent white and people in these ghettos viewed the police as an occupying army—much like the United States army that was occupying South Vietnam.

Eldridge Cleaver eloquently put these feelings into words. His comparisons of the police in Watts to the U.S. Army in Vietnam were taken to heart by blacks—and many whites. Cleaver's book *Soul on Ice* was written while the author was serving time in California's Folsom Prison for armed robbery. The essays on violence, race, and revolution were used as the founding philosophy of the Black Power movement. After his release from prison, Cleaver ran for president for the Peace and Freedom Party in 1968. In the 1980s, he renounced his Black Panther ethos and became a Republican and born-again Christian. Cleaver died in May 1998.

The police department and the armed forces are the two arms of the power structure, the muscles of control and enforcement. They have deadly weapons with which to in-

Excerpted from Eldridge Cleaver, *Soul on Ice*. Reprinted with permission from The McGraw-Hill Companies.

flict pain on the human body. They know how to bring about horrible deaths. They have clubs with which to beat the body and the head. They have bullets and guns with which to tear holes in the flesh, to smash bones, to disable and kill. They use force, to make you do what the deciders have decided you must do.

Every country on earth has these agencies of force. The people everywhere fear this terror and force. To them it is like a snarling wild beast which can put an end to one's dreams. They punish. They have cells and prisons to lock you up in. They pass out sentences. They won't let you go when you want to. You have to stay put until they give the word. If your mother is dying, you can't go to her bedside to say goodbye or to her graveside to see her lowered into the earth, to see her, for the last time, swallowed up by that black hole.

The techniques of the enforcers are many: firing squads, gas chambers, electric chairs, torture chambers, the garrote, the guillotine, the tightening rope around your throat. It has been found that the death penalty is necessary to back up the law, to make it easier to enforce, to deter transgressions against the penal code. That everybody doesn't believe in the same laws is beside the point.

Which laws get enforced depends on who is in power. If the capitalists are in power, they enforce laws designed to protect their system, their way of life. They have a particular abhorrence for crimes against property, but are prepared to be liberal and show a modicum of compassion for crimes against the person—unless, of course, an instance of the latter is combined with an instance of the former. In such cases, nothing can stop them from throwing the whole book at the offender. For instance, armed robbery with violence, to a capitalist, is the very epitome of evil. Ask any banker what he thinks of it.

If Communists are in power, they enforce laws designed to protect their system, their way of life. To them, the horror of horrors is the speculator, that man of magic who has mastered the art of getting something with nothing and who in America would be a member in good standing of his local Chamber of Commerce.

"The people," however, are nowhere consulted, although everywhere everything is done always in their name and ostensibly for their betterment, while their real-life problems go unsolved. "The people" are a rubber stamp for the crafty and sly. And no problem can be solved without taking the police department and the armed forces into account. Both kings and bookies understand this, as do first ladies and common prostitutes.

Protecting Those in Power

The police do on the domestic level what the armed forces do on the international level: protect the way of life for those in power. The police patrol the city, cordon off communities, blockade neighborhoods, invade homes, search for that which is hidden. The armed forces patrol the world, invade countries and continents, cordon off nations, blockade islands and whole peoples; they will also overrun villages, neighborhoods, enter homes, huts, caves, searching for that which is hidden. The policeman and the soldier will violate your person, smoke you out with various gases. Each will shoot you, beat your head and body with sticks and clubs, with rifle butts, run you through with bayonets, shoot holes in your flesh, kill you. They each have unlimited firepower. They will use all that is necessary to bring you to your knees. They won't take no for an answer. If you resist their sticks, they draw their guns. If you resist their guns, they call for reinforcements with bigger guns. Eventually they will come in tanks, in jets, in ships. They will not rest until you surrender or are killed. The policeman and the soldier will have the last word.

Both police and the armed forces follow orders. Orders. Orders flow from the top down. Up there, behind closed doors, in antechambers, in conference rooms, gavels bang on the tables, the tinkling of silver decanters can be heard as icewater is poured by well-fed, conservatively dressed men in hornrimmed glasses, fashionably dressed Ameri-

Demands from the Black Panther Party

When Huey Newton, Bobby Seale and others founded the Black Panther Party, they researched political theories on which to base their organization. Newton wrote the following list of demands as a basic platform for the party.

What We Want, What We Believe

1. We want freedom. We want power to determine the destiny of our black Community.

We believe that black people will not be free until we are free to determine our own destiny.

2. We want full employment for our people.

We believe that the federal government is responsible and obligated to give every man employment or a guaranteed income. We believe that if the white American businessman will not give full employment, then the means of production should be taken away from the businessman and placed in the community so that the people of the community can organize and employ all of its people and give a high standard of living.

3. We want an end to the robbery by the capitalists of our black community.

We believe that this racist government has robbed us and now we are demanding the overdue debt of forty acres and two mules. Forty acres and two mules were promised 100 years ago as restitution for slave labor and mass murder of black people. We will accept the payment in currency which will be distributed to our many communities. . . . The American racist has taken part in the slaughter of over fifty million black people; therefore, we feel that this is a modest demand that we make.

4. We want decent housing fit for shelter of human beings.

We believe that if the white landlords will not give decent housing to our black community, then the housing and the land should be made into cooperatives so that our community, with government aid, can build and make decent housing for its people.

5. We want education for our people that exposes the true nature of this decadent American society. We want education

*that teaches us our true history and our role in the present-
day society.*

6. We want all black men to be exempt from military service.

We believe that black people should not be forced to fight
in the military service to defend a racist government that
does not protect us. We will not fight and kill other people
of color in a world who, like black people, are victimized by
the white racist government of America. We will protect ourselves from the force and violence of the racist police and
the racist military, by whatever means necessary.

*7. We want an immediate end to POLICE BRUTALITY
and MURDER of black people.*

We believe we can end police brutality in our black community by organizing black self-defense groups that are dedicated to defending our black community from racist police
oppression and brutality. . . .

*8. We want freedom for all black men held in federal,
state, county and city prisons and jails.*

We believe that all black people should be released from
the many jails and prisons because they have not received a
fair and impartial trial. . . .

*9. We want all black people when brought to court to be
tried by a jury of their peer group from their black communities, as defined by the Constitution of the United States.*

We believe that the courts should follow the United States
Constitution so that black people will receive fair trials. . . .
To do this the court will be forced to select a jury from the
black community from which the black defendant came. We
have been and are being tried by all-white juries that have
no understanding of the "average reasoning man" of the
black community.

*10. We want land, bread, housing, education, clothing,
justice, and peace. And as our major political objective, a
United Nations–supervised plebiscite to be held throughout
the black colony in which only black colonial subjects will
be allowed to participate, for the purpose of determining the
will of black people as to their national destiny.*

Quoted in *The Shadow of the Panther: Huey Newton and the Price of Black Power in
America*. Reading, MA: Addison-Wesley Publishing, 1994.

can widows with rejuvenated faces and tinted hair, the air permeated with the square humor of Bob Hope jokes. Here all the talking is done, all the thinking, all the deciding. Gray rabbits of men scurry forth from the conference room to spread the decisions throughout the city, as News. Carrying out orders is a job, a way of meeting the payments on the house, a way of providing for one's kiddies. In the armed forces it is also a duty, patriotism. Not to do so is treason.

Equal Rights, Unequal Possessions

Every city has its police department. No city would be complete without one. It would be sheer madness to try operating an American city without the heat, the fuzz, the man. Americans are too far gone, or else they haven't arrived yet; the center does not exist, only the extremes. Take away the cops and Americans would have a coast-to-coast free-for-all. There are, of course, a few citizens who carry their own private cops around with them, built into their souls. But there is robbery in the land, and larceny, murder, rape, burglary, theft, swindles, all brands of crime, profit, rent, interest—and these blasé descendants of Pilgrims are at each other's throats. To complicate matters, there are also rich people and poor people in America. There are Negroes and whites, Indians, Puerto Ricans, Mexicans, Jews, Chinese, Arabs, Japanese—all with equal rights but unequal possessions. Some are haves and some are have-nots. All have been taught to worship at the shrine of General Motors. The whites are on top in America and they want to stay there, up there. They are also on top in the world, on the international level, and they want to stay up there, too. Everywhere there are those who want to smash this precious toy clock of a system, they want ever so much to change it, to rearrange things, to pull the whites down off their high horse and make them equal. Everywhere the whites are fighting to prolong their status, to retard the erosion of their position. In America, when everything else fails, they call out the police. On the international level, when everything else fails, they call out the armed forces.

A New War Cry

A strange thing happened in Watts, [during the riots] in 1965, August. The blacks, who in this land of private property have all private and no property, got excited into an uproar because they noticed a cop before he had a chance to wash the blood off his hands. Usually the police department can handle such flare-ups. But this time it was different. Things got out of hand. The blacks were running amok, burning, shooting, breaking. The police department was powerless to control them; the chief called for reinforcements. Out came the National Guard, that ambiguous hybrid from the twilight zone where the domestic army merges with the international; that hypocritical force poised within America and capable of action on either level, capable of backing up either the police or the armed forces. Unleashing their formidable firepower, they crushed the blacks. But things will never be the same again. Too many people saw that those who turned the other cheek in Watts got their whole head blown off. At the same time, heads were being blown off in Vietnam. America was embarrassed, not by the quality of her deeds but by the surplus of publicity focused upon her negative selling points, and a little frightened because of what all those dead bodies, on two fronts, implied. Those corpses spoke eloquently of potential allies and alliances. A community of interest began to emerge, dripping with blood, out of the ashes of Watts. The blacks in Watts and all over America could now see the Viet Cong's point: both were on the receiving end of what the armed forces were dishing out.

So now the blacks, stung by the new knowledge they have unearthed, cry out: *"POLICE BRUTALITY!"* From one end of the country to the other, the new war cry is raised. The youth, those nodes of compulsive energy who are all fuel and muscle, race their motors, itch to do something. The Uncle Toms [blacks who kowtow to whites], no longer willing to get down on their knees to lick boots, do so from a squatting position. The black bourgeoisie [middle class] call for Citizens' Review Boards, to assert civilian control over the activity of the police. In back rooms, in dark stinking corners of the ghettos, self-conscious black men curse their own cowardice and stare at their rifles and pistols and shotguns laid out on tables before them, trembling as they wish for a manly impulse to course through their bodies and send them screaming mad into the streets shooting from the hip. Black women look at their men as if they are bugs, curious growths of flesh playing an inscrutable waiting game. Violence becomes a homing pigeon floating through the ghettos seeking a black brain in which to roost for a season.

In their rage against the police, against police brutality, the blacks lose sight of the fundamental reality: that the police are only an instrument for the implementation of the policies of those who make the decisions. Police brutality is only one facet of the crystal of terror and oppression. Behind police brutality there is social brutality, economic brutality, and political brutality. From the perspective of the ghetto, this is not easy to discern: the TV newscaster and the radio announcer and the editorialists of the newspapers are wizards of the smoke screen and the snow job.

Only Following Orders

What is true on the international level is true also at home; except that the ace up the sleeve is easier to detect in the international arena. Who would maintain that American soldiers are in Vietnam on their own motion? They were conscripted into the armed forces and taught the wisdom of obeying orders. They were sent to Vietnam by orders of the generals in the Pentagon, who receive them from the Secretary of Defense, who receives them from the President, who is shrouded in mystery. The soldier in the field in Vietnam, the man who lies in the grass and squeezes the trigger when a little half-starved, trembling Vietnamese peasant crosses his sights, is only following orders, carrying out a policy and a plan. He hardly knows what it is all about. They have him wired-up tight with the slogans of TV and the World Series. All he knows is that he has been assigned to carry out a certain ritual of duties. He is well trained and does the best he can. He does a good job. He may want to please those above him with the quality of his performance. He may want to make sergeant, or better. This man is from some hicky farm in Shit Creek, Georgia. He only knew whom to kill after passing through boot camp. He could just as well come out ready to kill Swedes. He will kill a Swede dead if he is ordered to do so.

Same for the policeman in Watts. He is not there on his own. They have all been assigned. They have been told what to do and what not to do. They have also been told what they better not do. So when they continually do something, in every filthy ghetto in this shitty land, it means only that they are following orders.

Total Rebellion Against the System

It's no secret that in America the blacks are in total rebellion against the System. They want to get their nuts out of the sand. They don't like the way America is run, from top to bottom. In America, everything is owned. Everything is held as private property. Someone has a brand on everything. There is nothing left over. Until recently, the blacks themselves were counted as part of somebody's private property, along with the chickens and goats. The blacks have not forgotten this, principally because they are still treated as if they are part of someone's inventory of assets—or perhaps, in this day of rage against the costs of welfare, blacks are listed among the nation's liabilities. On any account, however, blacks are in no position to respect or help maintain the institution of private property. What they want is to figure out a way to get some of that property for themselves, to divert it to their own needs. This is what it is all about, and this is the real brutality involved. This is the source of all brutality.

The police are the armed guardians of the social order. The blacks are the chief domestic victims of the American social order. A conflict of interest exists, therefore, between the blacks and the police. It is not solely a matter of trigger-happy cops, of brutal cops who love to crack black heads. Mostly it's a job to them. It pays good. And there are numerous fringe benefits. The real problem is a trigger-happy social order.

The Utopians speak of a day when there will be no police. There will be nothing for them to do. Every man will do his duty, will respect the rights of his neighbor, will not disturb the peace. The needs of all will be taken care of. Everyone will have sympathy for his fellow man. There will be no such thing as crime. There will be, of course, no prisons. No electric chairs, no gas chambers. The hangman's rope will be the thing of the past. The entire earth will be a land of plenty. There will be no crimes against property, no speculation.

It is easy to see that we are not on the verge of entering Utopia: there are cops anywhere. North and South, the Negroes are the have-nots. They see property all around them, property that is owned by whites. In this regard, the black bourgeoisie has become nothing but a ridiculous nuisance. Having waged a battle for entrance into the American mainstream continually for fifty years, all of the black bourgeoisie's defenses are directed outward, against the whites. They have no defenses against the blacks and no time to erect any. The black masses can handle them any time they choose, with one mighty blow. But the white bourgeoisie presents a bigger problem, those whites who own everything. With many shackled by unemployment, hatred in black hearts for this system of private property increases daily. The sanctity surrounding property is being called into question. The mystique of the deed of ownership is melting away. In other parts of the world, peasants rise up and expropriate the land from the former owners. Blacks in America see that the deed is not eternal, that it is not signed by God, and that new deeds, making blacks the owners, can be drawn up. . . .

20 Million Strong

There are 20,000,000 of these blacks in America, probably more. Today they repeat, in awe, this magic number to themselves: there are 20,000,000 of us! They shout this to each other in humiliated astonishment. No one need tell them that there is vast power latent in their mass. They know that 20,000,000 of anything is enough to get some recognition and consideration. They know also that they must harness their number and hone it into a sword with a sharp cutting edge. White General Motors also knows that the unity of these 20,000,000 ragamuffins will spell the death of the system of its being. At all costs, then, they will seek to keep these blacks from uniting, from becoming bold and revolutionary. These white property owners know that they must keep the blacks cowardly and intimidated. By a complex communications system of hints and signals, certain orders are given to the chief of police and the sheriff, who pass them on to their men, the footsoldiers in the trenches of the ghetto. . . .

Meanwhile, blacks are looking on and asking tactical questions. They are asked to die for the System in Vietnam. In Watts they are killed by it. Now—*NOW!*—they are asking each other, in dead earnest: Why not die right here in Babylon fighting for a better life, like the Viet Cong? If those little cats can do it, what's wrong with big studs like us?

A mood sets in, spreads across America, across the face of Babylon, jells in black hearts everywhere.

Armed March on the California Statehouse

Bobby Seale

When researching political philosophies for the Black Panther Party, Huey Newton discovered an obscure California law (primarily for hunters) that allowed a person to carry a loaded shotgun or rifle providing that it was not concealed and was not pointed at another person. Because of alleged police brutality, the Black Panthers began to follow police patrols in black neighborhoods while carrying loaded weapons, claiming that they were acting in self defense.

When state legislator Donald Mulford proposed a law to make it illegal to carry loaded guns, the Panthers descended on the California statehouse in Sacramento dressed in black leather jackets, black berets, and fully armed with rifles and shotguns. As unbelievable as this seems in modern times, the Panthers were allowed in the legislative chambers. They later gave a news conference to state their positions on this and various other issues.

Bobby Seale was one of the founding members of the Black Panther Party in Oakland, California. In 1969, Seale was indicted for conspiracy to start a riot at the Democratic convention in Chicago. At the trial, because of his protests in the courtroom, Seale was bound and gagged. The image of this African American man, tied to his seat in a courtroom with a gag in his mouth, is one of the enduring images of the sixties.

In the following excerpt from his autobiography, Seale writes about leading the armed Panthers into the California statehouse that afternoon in 1967.

Excerpted from *A Lonely Rage,* by Bobby Seale (New York: Times Books, 1978). Copyright 1978 by Bobby Seale. Reprinted by permission of the author.

H uey [Newton] called me on the phone.

"Say, Bobby, ah, look, we've got to—better yet, come over here to my apartment. It's important. We got to make a special move."

"Right! On my way."

I hung up the phone, went out and hopped down the front steps into the Monday morning sun, . . . and drove up to Huey's apartment wondering what kind of special move we had to make, enthusiastically ready for the rundown.

I sat on the edge of the couch as Huey stood. He said, "Look, here in the papers. This guy, [Donald] Mulford, assemblyman at the state capital, is trying to get a bill in against us carrying guns."

I tried to speed-read the article as Huey went on.

"They're after us. The police are behind it. They calling us gun-toting bandits and the real reason is because we've made them respect us because of, ah, the way we're using the law—blowing it in their faces when we patrol them. They're mad and probably scared we'll blow their cracker asses away." Huey chuckled a bit, which made me feel a certain lightheartedness about it all: the fact that we weren't dead yet. I felt that after we had escorted [the widow of Malcolm X] Betty Shabazz [to the airport], stood off the San Francisco police, cordoned off a whole block out in North Richmond and dared the police to come up into that community after they had brutally murdered a brother named Denzil Dowell—because of this the Oakland police were venting their guilty racist asses to this jive assemblyman, Mulford.

I remembered how my Mama would say, "You always reap what you sow." And I looked at the brutalizing racist police as strictly being the cause of why we were revolutionaries—carrying guns, ready to blow their butts away at the slightest act of police brutality we may have caught them in.

"So look," Huey continued. "What we have to do is get ourselves, ah, more publicity explaining our political goals in the ten-point program."

"Yeah, ok."

"And what we have to do is go to the Capitol, armed, with

all the brothers. Look, they're out to get a law on the books to stop us from carrying *loaded* guns! So they can shoot us on sight and cut our program; and the press distorting will tell the black community that to arm yourselves is futile, and no one will see the actual political goals. We show the essence of the political power structure's farce when we patrol the police, showing the people; and, therefore, we've begun to show black people about their oppressed conditions."

"Yeah, I can dig the set."

No Alternative but to Shoot Back

We decided to draw up a position paper, get Eldridge Cleaver to write a mandate we could read to the press in Sacramento.

We talked with some others, and Eldridge brought up the idea that Huey should not go to Sacramento, being that he was the main head leader of the Black Panther Party for Self-Defense, and that going would be likely to result in being busted for parole reasons. Huey insisted that he had to go, but we outvoted him and insisted that he should not. I would go and read the statement. Then Huey wanted it noted that the meeting was composed of the five of us who comprised a sort of Party central body, agreeing and deciding to make the move.

With that settled, Huey ran down specific instructions to me; about the possibility of a leak getting out that we were headed to Sacramento and the police and/or National Guard being there. I was to read the statement *for sure* and leave. He said, "Don't go inside the Capitol. Do it on the front steps, and if you are challenged by any police shooting at us, then you have no alternative but to shoot back. But outside of that, take any arrests. We'd rather get our political point across than have a number of brothers shot up and killed."

"Right. I got you."

"Little Bobby," Huey added. "You stay close to Bobby. He's our chairman."

"Right," Little Bobby enthusiastically put in in a youthful upright manner. "Huey, Bobby, man! You-all some of the baddest motherfuckers I ever seen!"

We all filled our gas tanks up when the caravan stopped at the nearest gas station. Twenty brothers and five sisters. I told each driver, "Sacramento, the state capital—ready!"

After we got out of our cars in Sacramento, I gestured to them all to gather around me on the sidewalk area as they held their rifles and shotguns upright in a safety position. I spotted Eldridge, in a Panther uniform, moving around and clicking pictures in a hurry at all angles. Little Bobby handed me a stack of the mimeographed statements, which I glanced at and rolled up in the thin black leather glove of my left hand.

Shock and Fear

"Ok, everybody just stay sort of loosely near me. I mean, don't crowd me. And where there's press, then that's who I have to read this message to," I held the roll up in the air. "So let's stay together, ok?"

"Yeah, oh yeah!" and "Let's do it!"

"And tell these murdering dogs about *us* shooting *them* for a change!" the older Dowell brother spouted loudly in anger.

I spotted a tall, heavyset white man and his wife. They were stopped in their tracks, standing, staring at us. I raised my black-gloved hand up in the air.

"Ok, you-all! Let's move on out!" Pointing out the direction.

I took off walking, looking into the faces of the white man and woman who had stepped completely off the sidewalk and onto the grass, looking with their mouths wide open with shock and fear at all these niggers with guns. I had to smile.

Little Bobby was to my left and Orlando to my right. I glanced all around in back of me. Eldridge was flicking pictures. There were no smiles on the hard mean black faces of our thirty men and women. Yet, I knew these brothers, all of them. And most were really easy-going dudes, unless riled. Shit, black dudes off the block just *looked* rough. Damn! Huey was always telling me I looked mean. And I knew

God damn well I didn't even try to look mean. Maybe it came from trying to adopt the expressions I had seen in pictures of American Indians, I thought. Yeah, and it's their fight, too. They're on reservations: cooped up like black people in ghettos. I noticed white people passing and looking, most with awe on their faces.

I approached the first set of steps and saw the TV cameramen hustling toward us, and I stepped our crew to the top of the stairs and stopped as we met with the news.

An excited white reporter, microphone in hand, asked, "Black Panthers, right?" He gestured to the cameraman trying to situate his heavy camera.

"That's right." I spoke up sternly. "The Black Panther Party for Self-Defense." And I unrolled my stack of statements and handed him the mandate message and proceeded to read the message with force, light there in full view, glancing up from the page, noticing another camera had arrived. I felt the meaning behind the words, feeling myself reading a little too fast and slowing when I stumbled on a word or two.

"Bobby Seale, aren't you?" a reporter asked.

"Yeah, man." Five microphones were suddenly jammed up in my face and I unrolled the statements, kept four or five, and handed the rest to Little Bobby. "Tell Artie or somebody to pass these out to the reporters."

"Right!"

And I read the statement in full again.

"Are you going inside?" a reporter asked.

Then I remembered, from the movies I'd seen, that citizens had a spectators' section where they could watch the legislature in action. What are these cats called besides "assemblymen?" Are there two houses?

I was confused as a reporter said, "The assembly is in session. Bobby Seale, ah, is this a protest against Assemblyman Mulford's bill to stop this dangerous gun carrying by the Defense of the Black Panthers?"

The assembly was in session. I wanted to see—

Huey had told me don't go in, but everything had been so easy up to now.

10 TV Cameras, 50 Microphones

"Ok, let's go!" I shouted out, looking to see if they all heard me. I was surrounded and I stepped toward an open door and walked inside about twenty steps. I didn't know whether to go to my left, my right, or straight ahead down the long hall.

I spotted more white people, with their mouths hanging open. Their frightened, still expressions said, in my interpretation, "Niggers with guns—niggers with guns!" I felt they were just where I wanted them. I stepped off, deciding to go down the long hall, as the reporters scooted and rushed and hustled and bustled all around us; then cameramen and more reporters with microphones walked backwards, asking questions, filming, as our band of gun-toting, bandoliered, shotgun-, rifle-, and pistol-packing, mean-faced Party members put on the air of force and vigilance. Tired, angry warriors, brave warriors. I could feel the back-down caused by our surprise presence.

"Say, look," I asked a reporter. "Where is the assembly spectators' area?"

"You have to go upstairs," he excitedly answered.

"Ok, everybody, second floor."

Reporters jammed into the elevator trying to film and ask questions, guns and rifles mixed with several cameras and microphones were everywhere.

We took off walking again.

"This way, Bobby!" A reporter pointed and I walked, turning to my right, with some of our crew getting ahead of me.

"You going in, Bobby?" An excited, big-eyed reporter pointed to the wide door to the right. "Let's find the spectators' section."

They followed as I turned and stepped out the tall open door.

Some speaker bellowed on the microphone about assembly rules being broken. I turned, telling the brothers behind me to hold it, holding up my leather-gloved hand. "Wait! We in the wrong place!" "Bobby! Bobby!" Who was calling me? Oh—I spotted Eldridge. "The message," he said, "Read it!"

"Yeah, Bobby, read it, read it again." The reporters were shouting for me to do so. "We didn't get it!"

"Ok, ok, everybody! Hold down!" I demanded loudly, as I noticed at least ten TV cameras and what looked like fifty microphones all around. It got very quiet as I prepared myself to read the message.

"The Black Panther Party for Self-Defense calls upon the American people in general and black people in particular to take careful note of the racist California legislature now considering legislation aimed at keeping black people disarmed and powerless while racist police agencies—" And I read the whole message; the crowded quietness of the area making every word felt.

"Say look," I said after I'd finished, "are we under arrest or not!" I spoke directly to one of the guards who had surrounded us.

"No," he answered calmly, "you're not under arrest."

I stepped back and turned. "Ok, everybody. We splitting." I led the way. And we headed out, the reporters following us out to the front steps. Another cameraman ran up to me and asked me to read the statement once again. I did. And as fast as I finished, we moved out, headed for Oakland.

Face Off with a Traffic Cop

The hot Sacramento sun had me wanting to take off my black leather jacket as we walked on the twenty-foot-wide walkway. I stopped by the rear car, the shade of the trees easing the heat some.

"Ok, now, we headed back home," I told everyone. "We got a big lunch. A couple a big boxes of fried chicken and sandwiches some of the sisters from North Richmond put together. We'll eat lunch somewhere back on the highway."

We piled into our automobiles. At my direction, everyone was to follow my car and meet up with the other two cars around the neatly manicured park that looked to be the equivalent of ten square blocks.

Everyone now was complaining about the heat. My black leather jacket was hot. I wanted to take it off. I was about to turn right to head back toward the freeway, but when the green light came on, I changed my mind in a flash, after seeing the service station across the street. I drove straight across instead of turning right, and up into the service station alongside a pump.

"You-all use the toilet if you got to," I said. "I got to come out of this jacket and Tucker got to get some water for my old car." Opening the door, getting out, watching the last car park, I felt I should have turned to leave Sacramento.

Somebody was asking the white attendant for the keys to the restroom. Bobby and Orlando were hungry. Mark Comfort and Dowell had made their way across the station yard to me, guns in their hands.

"Hey," Mark said calmly. "Here come a jive cop. He's stopping."

I looked around to see a motorcycle cop. He looked from one end of the service station back to us. He got off his traffic cycle, an older cop in a blue short-sleeve uniform shirt. He stood looking, confused, then started walking down the sidewalk. I noticed he was pulling out his revolver as he slowly walked on with a not-knowing-what-to-do awe on his face to see five or six rifles in the brothers' hands, and suddenly a few brothers were opening doors, getting more rifles and shotguns out.

"Hey, Dowell Mark!" They came up behind me and walked with me. We were almost to the other cars. "Stay ready. Hey you-all, stay ready!"

I stepped toward the cop, dropping my hand down alongside the hand grip of my gun.

Clackup! I heard the sound of the brothers loading rounds into the chambers of a rifle and then a shotgun.

Am I Under Arrest?

I raised my left black-gloved hand up, palm open, at the cop, who was not aiming his gun, but now casually holding it up at me. His eyes, however, were looking beyond me as I could see cold red fear in them that said, "All these niggers with these guns! Where did they come from?"

"Say!" I hollered out. "Put that gun back in your holster!" I let an angry tone prevail so the brothers behind me would also hear.

God damn, these brothers is ready! A few were behind the hoods of cars and others had taken open-standing positions. *Clackup! Clackup!* Shit! I turned to look in the cop's face, my right hand now resting on the hand butt of my own forty-five.

He slowly raised his arm, putting his revolver back into his holster, letting his eyes catch mine. I realized it was black niggers, block brothers, versus white fear.

"Now. If you want to make an arrest, make it! But don't draw no gun on us at all! You got that?"

He looked at me as though he couldn't believe I was there telling him what he better or better not do.

"You draw a gun or shoot at us, you subject to get killed. But if you want to make an arrest, then say so! And we'll take the arrest. But keep your gun in your holster. And don't make no mistake about it. The right to self-defense is here! Are we under arrest?"

The radio spurted with static. We could hear a sudden excitement in the voice over the radio though the words weren't clear.

"Say you-all! Look, they want to arrest us. Now everybody remember, we take the arrest. Remember, we *take* the *arrest!*"

Five minutes later the corner service station was surrounded with cop cars. Some traffic was being redirected. I walked around the service station area repeating to everyone to take the arrest, we've broken no laws.

I was handcuffed and put into the back of a car. I noticed over half my crew was still armed, holding their guns in a proper upright manner. I saw Eldridge on the scene taking pictures. And then I was whisked away to the Sacramento city jail.

Out on bail, all the brothers were black heroes to all the women. A few sisters almost snatched brothers they knew inside and into the bedrooms, loving them. We were put on a pedestal as bad tough black men. We were admired to the hilt—while on the other hand, in the press, the Black Panther Party was referred to as a bunch of hoodlums. "Hoodlums Invade Capitol!"

Huey and I read the papers every day for five days. To the press and white politicians, we were all full of Lucifer. We found out we had hit the front page of the London *Times*. We were asked to appear on every radio and TV show.

The Black Panther Party for Self-Defense was now a household word in the Bay area, and its leaders were Huey Newton and Bobby Seale.

How to Run a Revolution

Huey Newton

Black Panther founder Huey Newton did not believe that
large-scale riots in African American neighborhoods would
help blacks achieve the revolutionary goals that he envisioned. Instead, Newton urged his followers to commit sabo-
tage and mayhem against "oppressors" in small groups that
could easily escape the police, whom he compared to the
World War II Nazi security officers known as the Gestapo.
Newton wrote the following article for the July 20, 1967, edi-
tion of the *Black Panther Newspaper*.

    Huey Newton was an activist at Merritt Junior College in
Oakland where he met Bobby Seale. Together they founded
the Black Panther Party for Self-Defense, with Seale acting as
chairman and Newton as Minister of Defense. In 1989 Newton was shot and killed by a drug dealer.

The Black masses are handling the resistance [to white
authority] incorrectly. When the brothers in East Oakland, having learned their resistance fighting from [the riots
in] Watts, amassed the people in the streets, threw bricks and
Molotov cocktails [bottles filled with gasoline] to destroy
property and create disruption, they were herded into a small
area by the . . . police and immediately contained by the brutal violence of the oppressor's storm troops. Although this
manner of resistance is sporadic, short-lived, and costly, it
has been transmitted across the country to all the ghettos of

Reprinted from Huey Newton, "Killuminati," *Black Panther Newspaper*, July 20, 1967.

the Black nation. The identity of the first man who threw a Molotov cocktail is not known by the masses, yet they respect and imitate his action. In the same way, the actions of the party will be imitated by the people—if the people respect these activities.

Revolution in Small Groups

The primary job of the [Black Panther] party is to provide leadership for the people. It must teach by words and action the correct strategic methods of prolonged resistance. When the people learn that it is no longer advantageous for them to resist by going into the streets in large numbers, and when they see the advantage in the activities of the guerrilla warfare method, they will quickly follow this example.

But first, [the people] must respect the party which is transmitting this message. When the vanguard group destroys the machinery of the oppressor by dealing with him in small groups of three and four, and then escapes the might of the oppressor, the masses will be impressed and more likely to adhere to this correct strategy. When the masses hear that a Gestapo policeman has been executed while sipping coffee at a counter, and the revolutionary executioners fled without being traced, the masses will see the validity of this kind of resistance. It is not necessary to organize thirty million Black people in primary groups of two's and three's, but it is important for the party to show the people how to stage a revolution. . . .

The main function of the party is to awaken the people and teach them the strategic method of resisting a power structure which is prepared not only to combat with massive brutality the people's resistance but to annihilate totally the Black population. If it is learned by the power structure that Black people have "X" number of guns in their possession, that information will not stimulate the power structure to prepare itself with guns; it is already prepared.

The end result of this revolutionary education will be positive for Black people in their resistance and negative for the power structure in its oppression because the party always exemplifies revolutionary defiance. If the party does not make the people aware of the tools and methods of liberation, there will be no means by which the people can mobilize. . . .

If the party machinery is to be effective it is important that the members of the party group maintain a face-to-face relationship with each other. . . . To minimize the danger of Uncle Tom informers and opportunists the members of the vanguard group should be tested revolutionaries.

The main purpose of the vanguard group should be to raise the consciousness of the masses through educational programs and other activities. The sleeping masses must be bombarded with the correct approach to struggle and the party must use all means available to get this information

Free Huey

Huey Newton's Black Panthers served free breakfasts for poor children and set up free clinics in Oakland's black ghetto. In 1967, Newton was sent to prison after a Black Panther confrontation with Oakland police left one officer dead. The Panthers began a national "Free Huey" campaign that became a celebrated cause with black and white radicals alike. In 1971, the California Court of Appeals reversed Newton's conviction and set him free. The following statement was released by The Central Committee of the Black Panther Party to facilitate Newton's release.

The Black Panther Party is informing and calling on all the peoples of the communities across the country to SCORN and DENOUNCE the actions of this capitalist-racist government's attempts to try and destroy the Black Panther Party which has chapters and branches across the nation. SCORN, DENOUNCE, and DESTROY the lies by capitalists and racists, from the Nixons, the Rockefellers, and all their pig lackeys, to the bootlicking cultural nationalists and black capitalists. They are the real conspirators where we see their obvious attempts to destroy the Black Panther Party's revolutionary leadership. They, of course, across to the masses. In order to do so the masses must know that the party exists. A vanguard party is never underground in the beginning of its existence; that would limit its effectiveness and educational goals. How can you teach people if the people do not know and respect you? The party must exist aboveground as long as the dog power structure will allow, and, hopefully, when the party is forced to go underground, the party's message will already have been put across to the people. The vanguard party's activities on the surface will necessarily be short-lived. Thus the party must make a tremendous impact upon the people before it is driven into secrecy. By that time the people will know the party exists and will seek further information about its ac-

try to do this by murders, jailings, unfair court trials, the forcing of Eldridge Cleaver into exile, and the temporary imprisonment of the Minister of Defense, Huey P. Newton in California. FREE HUEY. THE REVOLUTION IS HERE. We the people of the world must FREE HUEY AND ALL POLITICAL PRISONERS because if it wasn't for Huey P. Newton, free BREAKFAST FOR CHILDREN programs before school would not be spreading across the nation. If it wasn't for Huey P. Newton, the idea of having free medicine and FREE HEALTH CLINICS wouldn't be in the process of being implemented. If it wasn't for Huey P. Newton, the teaching that "it's not a race struggle, but a class struggle" would not begin to be understood. IF IT WASN'T FOR HUEY P. NEWTON, THE TEN POINT PLATFORM AND PROGRAM OF THE BLACK PANTHER PARTY WOULD NOT BE IN THE PROCESS OF BEING IMPLEMENTED, PRACTICAL SOCIALIST PROGRAMS FROM THE BLACK NATION IS WHERE IT'S AT, WHEN EVEN OTHER ETHNIC GROUPS COPY IT, AND THE PEOPLES OF THE WORLD KNOW THIS IS THEIR AND THAT IT'S RIGHT.

MIM Homepage, "April 27, 1969," http://www.etext.org/Politics/MIM/bpp/bpp270469_14.htm.

tivities if it is driven underground.

Many would-be revolutionaries work under the fallacious notion that the vanguard party should be a secret organization which the power structure knows nothing about, and that the masses know nothing about except for occasional letters that come to their homes by night. Underground parties cannot distribute leaflets announcing an underground meeting. Such contradictions and inconsistencies are not recognized by these so-called revolutionaries. They are, in fact, afraid of the very danger that they are asking the people to confront. These so-called revolutionaries want the people to say what they themselves are afraid to say, to do what they themselves are afraid to do. That kind of revolutionary is a coward and a hypocrite. A true revolutionary realizes that if he is sincere death is imminent. The things he is saying and doing are extremely dangerous. Without this realization it is pointless to proceed as a revolutionary.

If these impostors would investigate the history of revolution they would see that the vanguard group always starts out aboveground and is driven underground by the aggressor. The Cuban Revolution is an example: When Fidel Castro started to resist the butcher Batista and the American running dogs, he began by speaking publicly on the University of Havana campus. He was later driven to the hills. His impact upon the dispossessed people of Cuba was tremendous and his teachings were received with much respect. When he went into hiding, the Cuban people searched him out, going to the hills to find him and his band of twelve [supporters].

Guns, Hand Grenades, and Bazookas

Millions and millions of oppressed people may not know members of the vanguard party personally but they will learn of its activities and its proper strategy for liberation through an indirect acquaintance provided by the mass media. But it is not enough to rely on the media of the power structure; it is of prime importance that the vanguard party develop its own communications organ, such as a newspaper, and at the same time provide strategic revolutionary art, and destruction of the oppressor's machinery. For example in Watts the economy and property of the oppressor was destroyed to such an extent that no matter how the oppressor tried in his press to whitewash the activities of the Black brothers, the real nature and cause of the activity was communicated to every Black community. And no matter how the oppressor tried in his own media to distort and confuse the message of [Black Panther] Brother Stokely Carmichael, Black people all over the country understood it perfectly and welcomed it.

The Black Panther Party for Self-Defense teaches that, in the final analysis the guns, hand grenades, bazookas, and other equipment necessary for defense must be supplied by the power structure. As exemplified by the Vietcong, these weapons must be taken from the oppressor. Therefore, the greater the military preparation on the part of the oppressor, the greater the availability of weapons for the Black community. It is believed by some hypocrites that when the people are taught by the vanguard group to prepare for resistance, this only brings 'the man' down on them with increasing violence and brutality; but the fact is that when the man becomes more oppressive he only heightens the revolutionary fervor. So if things get worse for oppressed people they will feel the need for revolution and resistance. The people make revolution; the oppressors, by their brutal actions, cause resistance by the people. The vanguard party only teaches the correct methods of resistance.

The complaint of the hypocrites that the Black Panther Party for Self-Defense is exposing the people to deeper suffering is an incorrect observation. By their rebellions in the Black communities across the country the people have proved that they will not tolerate any more oppression by the racist dog police. They are looking now for guidance to extend and strengthen their resistance struggle. The vanguard party exemplify the characteristics that make them worthy of leadership.

Hispanic Revolutionaries

Carletta Fields

> The civil rights and Black Power movements inspired other minorities to form their own groups to fight repression and racism. Once such group was the Young Lords, an Hispanic group in Chicago. Their cause was the subject of a story by Carletta Fields, the Illinois Chapter Reporter for the *Black Panther Newspaper,* in the May 19, 1969 edition.

In this country where illegality is systematic and injustice deliberate, not only Black people but Brown people as well, suffer the brunt of repression. The American eagle, with its predatory instincts . . . and Miss Liberty, with her deliberate ruthlessness, tramples on those people they find it profitable to attack and crush. America compresses its oppressed between an atmosphere of vileness and a ground of hostile instability and dares them to challenge the mediums. The Young Lords Organization, a Latin-American revolutionary group who are working in Chicago, have dared to dispel the mediums; they are demanding an end to the injustices heaved upon Latin-American people.

Latin-American people in this country face some of the same problems that we, Black people face, i.e., inadequate food, indecent housing, irrelevant education, police brutality, and unemployment. And what are the Young Lords doing? They are working for adequate food, decent housing, relevant education, police brutality cessation, and employment for

Reprinted from Carletta Fields, "Persecution of the Young Lords," *Black Panther Newspaper,* May 19, 1969.

their people. The power structure would have these problems continue, as people who have little power to solve these problems are easy to exploit. The Young Lords, however, cannot be placed into this category because they are showing their people the strategic method to resist the oppressive forces of the power structure. This has made them the "enemy" to the power structure and the "friend" to all who desire an end to imperialism. The power structure's perception of them has resulted in them being harassed, arrested, beaten, and shot by the pigs who "protect and serve" (yes, protect capitalistic enterprises and serve us with arrest warrants, search warrants, subpoenas, summons, and the like).

Love of Liberation, Hatred of Oppression

On Sunday, April 4, one of the Young Lords, Manuel Ramos, Minister of Defense was killed and Ralph Rivera, Minister of Education was critically wounded. Yes these two were dedicating their lives to the revolutionary struggle. They were shot by pigs who made it their goal to deal with them as all protesting poor and exploited people are dealt

Black Power was not the only movement fighting repression and racism in the sixties. Hispanic groups, such as this one being addressed by American labor leader Cesar Chavez in 1969, were also speaking out and taking action.

with: elimination.

These brothers who sought to overtake those who have unjustly taken over, whose love was liberation and hate was oppression, whose bodies lie stiff and contorted, whose blood overflows the State of Illinois and surges into those adjacent states, whose words (Todo el poder a la genta—All power to the people) can be heard reverberating in response to the scream of the oppressed—these brothers we hold sacred; these brothers we hold dearest; these brothers we hold highest.

Presently facing many trumped up charges (such as mob action, disorderly conduct, inciting to riot, and everything else that is false) Chairman of the Young Lords, Cha Cha Jimenez is picked up at least once a week by the pigs. Many other Young Lords as well have been arrested on similar conspired charges. The news media and the pigs would have us believe that the Young Lords are a menacing gang, but we know otherwise. Their continuous community efforts have proven this. But the massive intimidations and negative propaganda have not made the Young Lords cease their struggle for the liberation of their people—quite the contrary. More determined than ever, they are now intensifying their efforts to see that the needs of their people are met.

Revolutionary Brothers

We ask the people to witness the Young Lords as they attempt to improve their community and place its control in the hands of the Latin-American people, to witness the pig persecution of those who believe that power should be vested in the people and not in minority enterprises. We call on the people to judge whether the struggle for justice now being waged by the Young Lords is invalid; whether the murder of one and the intended murder of the other is right. We call on the people to judge whether the Young Lords deserve such persecution.

Regarding you, the Young Lords, as our true revolutionary brothers, as our comrades, and as our allies, the Black Panther Party is working jointly with you to see that aggression is thwarted and suppression is ended.

Chronology

1960

February 1: The first sit-in by African Americans is staged at a whites-only lunch counter at a Woolworth's in Greensboro, North Carolina.

November: John F. Kennedy is elected president.

Envoid, the first birth-control pill is approved by the Federal Drug Administration.

1961

May: Busloads of black and white civil rights workers, called Freedom Riders, travel through the South demanding an end to segregation on interstate bus travel; the U.S. supplies the South Vietnamese army with thirty-six helicopters and four hundred American advisers, providing direct military support for the first time.

1962

September: Black air force veteran James Meredith becomes the first African American student to enroll at the University of Mississippi. He begins classes under the protection of U.S. Marshals.

October: When the United States discovers that the Soviet Union is building nuclear missile launch sites in Cuba, the Cuban Missile Crisis erupts, threatening all-out nuclear war between the superpowers. The crisis ends six days later when the Soviets remove their missiles.

Ken Kesey's book *One Flew over the Cuckoo's Nest* is published. Kesey wrote the book based on his experiences while high on LSD at his job in a mental institution.

1963

August 28: Martin Luther King Jr. gives his "I Have a Dream" speech during the March on Washington.

November 22: President John F. Kennedy is assassinated in Dallas, Texas. Lyndon Johnson becomes the president of the United States.

Betty Friedan's *The Feminine Mystique,* a groundbreaking book about women's lack of equal rights, is published.

1964

February 9: The Beatles visit the United States for the first time and appear on the popular *Ed Sullivan Show.* Several of their songs soar to the top of the charts and they become the most popular band in America.

August 2–7: President Lyndon Johnson uses an alleged naval skirmish in Vietnam between the North Vietnamese and the U.S. Navy to begin a massive military campaign in Indochina.

November: Johnson is elected president for the first time after finishing the rest of assassinated president John F. Kennedy's term.

December 2: About fifteen hundred students take over campus administration buildings at the University of California at Berkeley to protest restrictions on free speech.

The Civil Rights Act of 1964, prohibiting discrimination on the basis of race, is passed by Congress.

Martin Luther King Jr. wins the Nobel Peace Prize.

Timothy Leary publishes *The Psychedelic Experience,* which popularizes his experiences with LSD.

1965

February 21: Malcolm X is assassinated at a Nation of Islam rally in New York City. His autobiography is published later that year.

March 8: The first American combat troops arrive in South Vietnam.

August 11–16: The Watts neighborhood, an African American section of Los Angeles, erupts in a five-day riot after white police officers beat a black motorist.

October 15: The first massive antiwar protests are held across the U.S. after American planes bomb North Vietnam; the first psychedelic party is held in San Francisco as hundreds of people take LSD and listen to rock bands.

Congress makes the burning of draft cards illegal.

1966

January: Ken Kesey holds the first of many "Acid Tests" where attendees take LSD, watch light shows, and dance to San Francisco's finest rock bands.

October 6: The federal law making the possession of LSD illegal goes into effect.

The National Organization for Women (NOW) is founded by Betty Friedan and others.

Huey Newton and Bobby Seale found the Black Panther Party in Oakland, California.

1967

January 14: Twenty thousand hippies invade Golden Gate Park for "the gathering of the tribes" or "Human Be-In."

Major media outlets in the United States file hundreds of stories about hippies in San Francisco, prompting thousands of people to converge on that city for what later would be called "the Summer of Love."

June: Former soldiers who fought in Indochina form the Vietnam Veterans Against the War organization.

October 21–23: Over fifty thousand anti–Vietnam War demonstrators protest at the Lincoln Memorial in Washington, D.C.; Abbie Hoffman and other war protesters surround the Pentagon and attempt to levitate the building into the air to "shake out the evil spirits."

1968

January 30–31: North Vietnamese soldiers stage a large-scale campaign known as the Tet Offensive. Though American troops turn back the invasion, the attack convinces many Americans that North Vietnam is far from defeated.

April 4: Martin Luther King Jr. is assassinated in Memphis, Tennessee. Race riots erupt across America.

June 6: Robert F. Kennedy is assassinated in Los Angeles after winning the California Democratic primary.

The Youth International Party, or Yippie, is formed by Abbie Hoffman, Jerry Rubin, and others.

August 26–29: The Democratic National Convention is held in Chicago. When tens of thousands of antiwar protesters arrive in the city, police beat and gas them along with members of the press and convention delegates.

November: Richard Nixon is elected president.

December: The bloodiest year of the Vietnam War sees 14,314 Americans killed and 150,000 wounded while 500,000 U.S. troops are stationed in Indochina.

Eldridge Cleaver's prison writing *Soul on Ice* is published.

1969

August 15–17: The Woodstock Music and Art Fair attracts around four hundred thousand people to Bethel, New York, for three days of peace, love, and music featuring acts such as Janis Joplin, Jimi Hendrix, the Who, and the Grateful Dead.

Abbie Hoffman, Jerry Rubin, Bobby Seale, Tom Hayden, and others known as the Chicago Seven are indicted on charges for conspiring to incite a riot at the 1968 Democratic National Convention.

For Further Research

Joan Baez, *And a Voice to Sing With.* New York: New American Library, 1987.

Warren J. Belasco, *Appetite for Change: How the Counterculture Took on the Food Industry.* New York: Pantheon Books, 1989.

Lenny Bruce, *How to Talk Dirty and Influence People.* New York: AMS, 1972.

Neil Cassady, *The First Third.* San Francisco: City Lights Books, 1981.

Sherri Cavan, *Hippies of the Haight.* St. Louis: New Critics, 1972.

Ronald Chepesiuk, *Sixties Radicals, Then and Now: Candid Conversations with Those Who Shaped the Era.* Jefferson, NC: McFarland, 1995.

Eldridge Cleaver, *Soul on Ice.* New York: Dell, 1992.

Jonathan Cott and Christina Doudna, eds., *The Ballad of John and Yoko.* Garden City, NY: Rolling Stone, 1982.

Stanley Crouch, *The Sixties: The Decade Remembered Now by the People Who Lived Then.* New York: Rolling Stone, 1977.

Editors of Time-Life Books, *Turbulent Years: The Sixties.* Alexandria, VA: Time-Life Books, 1998.

David Farber, *The Age of Great Dreams: America in the 1960s.* New York: Hill and Wang, 1994.

Betty Friedan, *The Feminine Mystique.* New York: Norton, 1963.

———, *It Changed My Life: Writings on the Women's Movement.* New York: Random House, 1976.

Todd Gitlin, *The Sixties: Years of Hope, Days of Rage.* New York: Bantam Books, 1987.

David Lance Goines, *The Free Speech Movement: Coming of Age in the 1960s.* Berkeley, CA: Ten Speed, 1993.

Robert Greenfield, *Dark Star: An Oral Biography of Jerry Garcia.* New York: William Morrow, 1996.

Emmett Grogan, *Ringolevio: A Life Played for Keeps.* New York: Citadel Underground Books, 1990.

David Harris, *Our War: What We Did in Vietnam and What It Did to Us.* New York: Times Books, 1996.

Hank Harrison, *The Dead Book.* New York: Links Books, 1973.

Tom Hayden, *Reunion: A Memoir.* New York: Random House, 1988.

William Hedgepeth, *The Alternative: Communal Life in New America.* New York: Macmillan, 1970.

Abbie Hoffman, *Soon to Be a Major Motion Picture.* New York: Perigee Books, 1980.

Peter Joseph, *Good Times: An Oral History of America in the Nineteen Sixties.* New York: Charterhouse, 1973.

Charles Kaiser, *1968 in America.* New York: Weidenfeld & Nicolson, 1988.

Linda Kelly, *Deadheads: Stories from Fellow Artists, Friends, and Followers of the Grateful Dead.* Secaucus, NJ: Carol, 1995.

Ken Kesey, *One Flew over the Cockoo's Nest.* New York: Viking, 1966.

Jesse Kornbluth, *New Notes from the Underground.* New York: Viking Press, 1968.

Timothy Leary, *The Politics of Ecstasy.* Berkeley, CA: Ronin, 1998.

John Lennon, *In His Own Write and a Spaniard in the Works.* New York: New American Library, 1967.

Malcolm X, as told to Alex Haley, *The Autobiography of Malcolm X.* New York: Ballantine Books, 1992.

Ray Manzarek, *Light My Fire: My Life with the Doors*. New York: G.P. Putnam, 1998.

James Miller, *"Democracy in the Streets" from Port Huron to the Siege of Chicago*. New York: Simon and Schuster, 1987.

Hugh Pearson, *The Shadow of the Panther: Huey Newton and the Price of Black Power in America*. Reading, MA: Addison-Wesley, 1994.

Charles Perry, *Twenty Years of Rolling Stone: What a Long, Strange Trip It's Been*. Ed. Jann Wenner. New York: Straight Arrow, 1987.

Helen Swick Perry, *The Human Be-In*. New York: Basic Books, 1970.

Jerry Rubin, *Do It!* New York: Ballantine Books, 1970.

Bobby Seale, *A Lonely Rage*. New York: Times Books, 1978.

Larry Sloman, *Steal This Dream: Abbie Hoffman and the Counterculture Revolution in America*. New York: Doubleday, 1998.

Richard Stacewicz, *Winter Soldiers: An Oral History of Vietnam Veterans Against the War*. New York: Twayne, 1997.

Jane and Michael Stern, *Sixties People*. New York: Alfred A. Knopf, 1990.

Jay Stevens, *Storming Heaven: LSD and the American Dream*. New York: Harper & Row, 1988.

Hunter S. Thompson, *Fear and Loathing in Las Vegas and Other American Stories*. New York: Modern Library, 1996.

Irwin Unger and Debi Unger, eds., *The Times Were a Changin': The Sixties Reader*. New York: Three Rivers, 1998.

Nicholas Von Hoffman, *We Are the People Our Parents Warned Us Against*. Chicago: Quadrangle Books, 1968.

Rex Weiner and Deanne Stillman, *Woodstock Census: The Nationwide Survey of the Sixties Generation.* New York: Viking, 1979.

Peter O. Whitmer with Bruce Van Wyngarden, *Aquarius Revisited: Seven Who Created the Sixties Counterculture and Changed America.* New York: Macmillan, 1987.

Jon Wiener, *Come Together: John Lennon in His Own Time.* New York: Random House, 1984.

Nancy Zaroulis and Gerald Sullivan, *Who Spoke Up? American Protest Against the War in Vietnam, 1963–1975.* Garden City, NY: Doubleday, 1984.

Web Sites

Carletta Fields, MIM's Black Panther Newspaper Collection, "May 19, 1969, Page 14." www.etext.org/Politics/MIM/bpp/bpp190569_14.htm.

MIM Homepage, "April 27, 1969," www.etext.org/Politics/MIM/bpp/bpp270469_14.htm.

Huey Newton, "The Correct Handling of a Revolution, Black Panther Newspaper, July 20, 1967." www.geocities.com/Area51/Vault/9516/hpn.html.

Valerie Solanas, *The S.C.U.M. Manifesto—Valerie Solanas.* www.bcn.net/~jpiazzo/scum.htm.

Stew Albert's Yippie Reading Room, "Abbie Hoffman Visits the Stock Exchange and Some Other Places," November 1999. http://hometown.aol.com/stewa/Abbiestock.html.

Youth International Party Resource Site, 1999. www.freespeech.org/yippie/index.htm.

Index